博雅 **CLI** 21世纪内容语言融合（CLI）系列英语教材

国家社会科学基金项目成果
高等教育国家级教学成果奖获奖项目成果
辽宁省普通高等教育本科教学成果奖获奖项目成果

英 国 国 情
英国社会与文化

（第3版）

UNDERSTANDING THE U.K.
SOCIETY AND CULTURE

(THIRD EDITION)

常俊跃 李莉莉 赵永青 主编

U0362552

北京大学出版社
PEKING UNIVERSITY PRESS

图书在版编目 (CIP) 数据

英国国情：英国社会与文化 / 常俊跃，李莉莉，赵永青主编 . —— 3 版 . —— 北京：北京大学出版社，2025. 2. —— （21 世纪内容语言融合（CLI）系列英语教材）. —— ISBN 978-7-301-35956-3

Ⅰ . H319.37

中国国家版本馆 CIP 数据核字第 2025UK0143 号

书　　　名	英国国情：英国社会与文化（第3版）
	YINGGUO GUOQING：YINGGUO SHEHUI YU WENHUA（DI-SAN BAN）
著作责任者	常俊跃　李莉莉　赵永青　主编
责 任 编 辑	李　颖
标 准 书 号	ISBN 978-7-301-35956-3
出 版 发 行	北京大学出版社
地　　　址	北京市海淀区成府路 205 号　100871
网　　　址	http://www.pup.cn　新浪微博：@ 北京大学出版社
电 子 邮 箱	编辑部 pupwaiwen@pup.cn　总编室 zpup@pup.cn
电　　　话	邮购部 010-62752015　发行部 010-62750672　编辑部 010-62754382
印 刷 者	河北博文科技印务有限公司
经 销 者	新华书店
	787 毫米 ×1098 毫米　16 开本　12 印张　438 千字
	2010 年 1 月第 1 版　2016 年 8 月第 2 版
	2025 年 2 月第 3 版　2025 年 2 月第 1 次印刷
定　　　价	49.00 元

第3版前言

长期以来,"以语言技能训练为导向"(Skill-Oriented Instruction,SOI)的教学理念主导了我国高校外语专业教育,即通过开设语音、语法、基础英语、高级英语、听力、口语、阅读、写作、翻译等课程进行语言教学,帮助学生提高语言技能。该理念对强化学生的语言技能具有一定的积极作用,但也导致了学生知识面偏窄、思辨能力偏弱、综合素质偏低等问题。

为了探寻我国外语专业教育的新路,大连外国语大学英语专业教研团队在总结西南联大等高校外语教育经验的基础上,在北美内容依托教学(Content-Based Instruction,CBI)的启发下,于2006年开展了校级和省级英语专业课程改革项目,还于2007—2022年连续开展了三个国家哲学社科项目,系统推进英语专业课程体系改革探索,推出中国特色鲜明的内容语言融合教育理念(Content and Language Integration,CLI),即"将目标语用于教授、学习内容和语言这两个重点,达到多种教育目的的教育理念"。CLI不仅具有自己独特的育人观、课程观、教材观、教学观、测评观、教师发展观,而且展示了如下特点:

1. **教育目标** 有别于诸多外语教学理念,CLI不局限于语言教学,而是服务知识、能力和素质培养三大目标,将价值塑造、知识传授和能力培养三者融为一体,寓价值观引导于知识传授和能力培养之中,帮助学生塑造正确的世界观、人生观、价值观,着力落实立德树人根本任务。知识目标包含专业知识、相关专业知识、跨学科知识;能力目标包含语言能力、认知能力、交际能力、思辨能力等;素质目标包含世界观、人生观、价值观、人文修养、国际视野、中国情怀、责任感、团队意识等。

2. **教学特点** 有别于单纯训练语言的教学,CLI指导下的语言训练依托内容,内容教学依靠语言;语言、内容融合教学,二者不再人为割裂。

3. **师生角色** 有别于传统教学和学生中心理念对师生角色的期待,CLI倡导在充分发挥教师主导作用的同时发挥学生的主体作用。教师可以扮演讲授者、评估者、建议者、资源提供者、组织者、帮助者、咨询者,同时也不排斥教师的权威角色等角色。学生角色也更加多元,包括学习者、参与者、发起者、创新者、研究者、问题解决者。

4. **教学材料** 有别于我国传统的外语教科书,在CLI指导下开发的教材具有多样化的特点,包括课本、音频资料、视频资料、网站资料、教学课件、学生作品等。教材的每个单元都围绕内容主题设计,内容具有连续性和系统性。

5. **教学侧重** CLI倡导教师要根据教学阶段或教学内容的特点确定教学重点,或侧重语言知识教学,或侧重语言技能教学,或侧重专业知识教学,或在语言教学和内容教学中达成某种平衡。

6. **教学活动** CLI主张教学活动不局限于某一种教学方法所规定的某几种技巧,倡导充分吸收各种教学方法促进语言学习、内容学习、素质培养的技巧,运用多种教学手段,通过问题驱动、输出驱动等方法调动学生主动学习;运用启发式、任务式、讨论式、结对子、小组活动、课堂展示、项目依托教学等行之有效的方法、活动与学科内容教学有机结合,提高学生的语言技能,激发学生的学习兴趣,培养学生的自主性和创造性,提升学

生的思辨能力和综合素质。

7. **教学测评** CLI主张测评要吸收测试研究和评价研究的成果,开展形成性评价和终结性评价。形成性评价可以有小测验、课堂发表、角色扮演、小组活动、双人活动、项目、撰写论文、撰写研究报告、创意写作、创意改写、反馈性写作、制作张贴作品等;终结性评价可以包括传统的选择题等各种测评方法。

8. **互动性质** CLI有别于传统教学从教师向学生的单向信息传送,课堂互动包括师生互动基础上的生生互动、生师互动乃至师生与其他人员的互动。

9. **情感处理** CLI重视对学生的人文关怀,主张教师关注学生的情感反应,教学中有必要有效处理影响学生学习的各种情感因素。

10. **母语作用** CLI尊重外语环境下师生的母语优势并加以利用。不绝对禁止母语的使用,母语的使用取决于教学的需要,母语用于有效支持教育目标的达成。

11. **应对失误** CLI认可失误是学生获得语言或知识内容不可避免的现象,对学生的失误采取包容的态度。针对具体情况应对学生的失误,或不去干预,允许学生自我纠正,或有针对性地适时给予纠正。

12. **理论支撑** CLI得到语言、认知、社会互动、学习等多种理论的支撑。包括:语言是以文本或话语为基础的;语言的运用借助各种技能的融合;语言具有目的性;当人们把语言当成获取信息的工具而不是目的时学习语言更成功,作为语言学习的基础使得一些内容比另外一些内容更有用;当教学关注学生的需求时学生的学习效果会更好;教学应该以学生以前的学习经历为基础。

在CLI指导下,依托三个国家哲学社科项目,我们将教育部《高等学校英语专业英语教学大纲》规定的语言技能课程(包括英语语音、英语语法、英语听力、英语口语、英语阅读、英语写作、基础英语、高级英语、英语视听说、英汉笔译、英汉口译等)和专业知识课程(包括英语国家概况、英国文学、美国文学、语言学概论、学术论文写作)进行系统改革,构建了全新的英语专业课程体系,包括九个系列的核心课程:

1. 提高综合英语能力的课程包括:美国文学经典作品、英国文学经典作品、世界文学经典作品、西方思想经典。依托美国、英国、世界的英语文学作品经典和西方思想经典的内容,提高学生综合运用英语的能力,丰富对文学及西方思想的认知,提高综合能力和综合素养。

2. 提高英语视听说能力的课程包括:美国社会文化经典电影、英国社会文化经典电影、环球资讯、专题资讯。依托美英社会文化经典电影、环球资讯、专题资讯内容,提高学生的英语听说能力,同时增加学生对相关国家社会文化的了解。

3. 提高英语口语表达的课程包括:功能英语交际、情景英语交际、英语演讲、英语辩论。依托人际交往的知识内容,提高学生的英语口语交际能力,增进对人际沟通的了解。

4. 提高英语写作能力的课程包括:段落写作、篇章写作、创意写作、学术英语写作。依托笔头交际的知识内容,提高学生的英语笔头表达能力。

5. 提高英汉互译能力的课程包括:英汉笔译、汉英笔译、交替传译、同声传译、专题口译。依托相关学科领域的知识内容,提高学生的英汉汉英笔译、交译、同传、专题口译技能,增加学生对相关领域的了解。

6. 拓展社会文化知识的课程:美国社会与文化、美国自然人文地理、美国历史文化、英国社会与文化、英国自然人文地理、英国历史文化、澳新加社会与文化、欧洲文化、中国文化、古希腊罗马神话、《圣经》与文化、跨文化交际。依托相关国家区域的社会、文化、史地等知识,扩展学生的社会文化知识,增加学生专业知识的系统性,拓宽学生的国际视野,同时提高学生的英语能力。

7. 提升英语文学修养的课程包括：英语短篇小说、英语长篇小说、英语散文、英语戏剧、英语诗歌。依托各种体裁的优秀文学作品内容，强化学生对英语文学文本的阅读，提高学生的文学欣赏能力及语言表达能力，提升学生的文学素养。

8. 提升语言理论修养的课程包括：英语语言学、英语词汇学、语言与社会、语言与文化、语言与语用。依托英语语言学知识内容，帮助学生深入了解英语语言，增加对语言与社会、文化、语用关系的认识，同时提升学生的专业表达能力。

9. 提升区域国别问题探究能力的课程包括：欧洲英语国家研究、北美英语国家研究、大洋洲英语国家研究、拉美英语国家研究、亚洲英语国家研究、非洲英语国家研究。通过指导学生获取区域国别学知识、开展区域国别问题研究项目，提高学生获取国情区情知识、拓宽国际视野、探究国别问题、进行语言沟通等综合能力和综合素养。

研究表明，CLI指导下的课程改革对学生的语音、词汇、语法、听力、口语、写作、交际、思辨、情感、知识等诸多方面产生了显著的积极影响。此外，对学生的研究、创新等能力也产生了积极影响。

CLI教育理念及其指导下的实践探索成果在国内外研讨会进行交流，产生了广泛的积极影响。CLI教育理念指导下开发的系列课程和教材在北京大学出版社、上海外语教育出版社等出版社出版并被广泛使用。培育的校级、省级和国家级教学研究成果在我国高校被广泛借鉴，出版的教学研究著作及在国内外学术期刊发表的研究论文对推进外语专业教育理念变革、改善教学实践发挥了积极的作用。高校教师积极参与CLI教育教学研讨与交流，200多所高校引进了理念、课程、教材并结合本校实际开展了课程改革，取得了积极成果。

该理念不仅得到一线教师的广泛支持，也得到了戴炜栋、王守仁、文秋芳等知名专家的高度肯定。蔡基刚教授认为其具有"导向性"作用。孙有中教授认为，该理念指导的教学改革"走在了全国的前列"。教育部前外语教学指导委员会主任委员戴炜栋建议推广探索的课程。内容语言融合教育理念被作为教学要求写入《外国语言文学类教学质量国家标准》及《普通高等学校本科英语类专业教学指南》，用于指导全国的外语专业教育，必将对我国的外语教育产生更大的影响。

《英国国情：英国社会与文化》是CLI教育理念指导下英语专业知识课程体系中英国社会与文化课程所使用的教材。教材针对的学生群体是具有中学英语基础的大学生，适用于英语专业一、二年级学生，也适用于具有中学英语基础的非专业学生和英语爱好者。总体看来，本教材具有以下主要特色：

1. 打破了传统的教学理念。本教材改变了"为学语言而学语言"的传统教材建设理念，在具有时代特色且被证明行之有效的内容依托教学理论指导下，改变了片面关注语言知识和语言技能忽视内容学习的做法。它依托学生密切关注的西方文明和文化内容，结合社会文化内容组织学生进行语言交际活动，在语言交流中学习有意义的知识内容，既训练语言技能，也丰富相关知识，起到的是一箭双雕的作用。

2. 涉及了丰富的教学内容。《英国国情：英国社会与文化》共分为十五个单元。教材以英国社会文化为主线，涉及英国人的性格、政治政体、饮食文化、行为礼仪、学校教育、社会福利、大众媒体、法律体系、家庭生活、体育竞技、风俗节日、文学艺术等主题。围绕大学生感兴趣的话题组织教材，帮助学生了解英国社会文化，正确认识英国社会文化，培养学生对异域社会文化的敏感性和包容态度，培养学生的国际视野。

3. 引进了真实的教学材料。英语教材是英语学习者英语语言输入和相关知识输入的重要渠道。本教材使用大量真实、地道的语言材料，为学生提供了高质量的语言输入。此外，为了使课文内容更加充实生动，易于学生理解接受，编者在课文中穿插了大量的插图、表格、照片等真实的视觉材料,表现手段活泼,形式多种多样,效果生动直观。

4. 设计了新颖的教材板块。本教材每一单元的主体内容均包括 Before You Read,Start to Read,After You Read 和 Read More 四大板块,不仅在结构上确立了学生的主体地位,而且系统的安排也方便教师借助教材有条不紊地开展教学活动。它改变了教师单纯灌输、学生被动接受的教学方式,促使学生积极思考、提问、探索、发现、批判,培养自主获得知识、发现问题和解决问题的能力。

5. 提供了有趣的训练活动。为了培养学生的语言技能和综合素质,本教材在关注英语语言知识训练和相关知识内容传授的基础上精心设计了生动多样的综合训练活动,例如头脑风暴、话题辩论、角色表演、主题陈述、故事编述等等。多样化的活动打破了传统教材单调的训练程式,帮助教师设置真实的语言运用情境,组织富于挑战性的、具有意义的语言实践活动,培养学生语言综合运用能力。

6. 推荐了经典的学习材料。教材的另一特色在于它对教学内容的延伸和拓展。在每个章节的最后部分,编者向学生推荐经典的书目、影视作品、名诗欣赏以及英文歌曲等学习资料,这不仅有益于学生开阔视野,也使教材具有了弹性和开放性,方便不同院校不同水平学生的使用。

本教材是我国英语专业综合课程改革的一项探索,凝聚了全体编写人员的艰苦努力。然而由于水平有限,还存在疏漏和不足,希望使用本教材的老师和同学们能为我们提出宝贵意见和建议。您的指导和建议将是我们提高的动力。

编者
2024 年 12 月 17 日
于大连外国语大学

目录

Unit 1

The English Character

> Success is the ability to go from one failure to another with no loss of enthusiasm.
>
> —Winston Churchill

Unit Goals

- To understand the character of English people
- To get acquainted with some basic cultural concepts concerning the English character
- To develop critical thinking and intercultural communication skills
- To learn useful words and expressions concerning the English character and improve English language skills

Before You Read

Work with your partner and share ideas with each other.

1) What are the first three things that come into your mind when you hear the word "Britain" or "Britons"?

   e.g. When I think of "Britain," I think of...

   _____

   _____

   _____

   _____

   _____

   _____

   _____

2) What do you think of the Britons? What are the three descriptive words you associate most with British people?

____ , ____ , ____

Start to Read

Text A　　The English Character (I)

1 To other Europeans, the best known quality of the British, and in particular of the English, is "**reserved**." A reserved person is one who does not talk very much to strangers, does not show much emotion, and seldom gets excited. It is difficult to get to know a reserved person: he never tells you anything about himself, and you may work with him for years without even knowing where he lives, how many children he has, and what his interests are. English people tend to be like that.

32 The British Character. Love of travelling alone.

Punch, 4 August 1937

2 If they are making a journey by bus, they will do their best to find an empty seat; if by train, an empty **compartment**. If they have to share the compartment with a stranger, they may travel many miles without starting a conversation. If a conversation does start, personal questions like "How old are you?" or even "What is your name?" are not easily asked.

3 This **reluctance** to communicate with others is an unfortunate quality in some ways since it tends to give the impression of coldness, and it is true that the English (except perhaps those in the North) are not noted for their **generosity** and **hospitality**. On the other hand, they are perfectly human behind their **barrier** of reserve, and may be quite pleased when a friendly stranger or foreigner succeeds for a time in breaking the barrier down. We may also mention at this point that the people of the North and West, especially the Welsh, are much less reserved than those of the South and the East.

4 Closely related to English reserve is English **modesty**. Within their hearts, the English are perhaps no less **conceited** than anybody else, but in their relations with others they value at least a show of modesty. Self-praise is felt to be impolite. If a person is, let us say, very good at tennis and someone asks him if he is a good player, he will seldom reply "Yes" because people will think him conceited. He will probably give an answer like "I'm not bad" or "I think I'm very good" or "Well, I'm very keen on tennis." Even if he had managed to reach the finals in last year's local **championships**, he would say it in such a way as to suggest that it was only due to a piece of good luck.

5 The famous English sense of humor is similar. Its starting-point is self-**dispraise**, and its great enemy is conceit. Its object is the ability to laugh at oneself—

at one's own faults, one's own failure, even at one's own ideals. The **criticism** "He has no sense of humor" is very commonly heard in Britain, where humor is highly prized. A sense of humor is an attitude to life rather than the mere ability to laugh at jokes. This attitude is never cruel or **disrespectful** or **malicious**. The English do not laugh at a cripple or a madman, or a tragedy or an honorable failure.

"The tooth has to come out anyway, no reason why we can't have a little fun."

6 Since reserve, a show of modesty and a sense of humor are part of his own nature, the typical Englishman tends to expect them in others. He secretly looks down on more **excitable** nations, and likes to think of himself as more reliable than them. He does not trust big promises and open shows of feelings, especially if they are expressed in **flowery** language. He does not trust self-praise of any kind. This applies not only to what other people may tell him about themselves orally, but to the letters they may write to him. To those who are fond of flowery expressions, the Englishman may appear uncomfortably cold.

P. BYRNES.

"Just remember, son, it doesn't matter whether you win or lose—unless you want Daddy's love."

7 Finally, **sportsmanship**. Like a sense of humor, this is an English ideal which not all Englishmen live up to. It must be realized that sport in this modern form is almost entirely a British invention. Boxing, rugby, football, hockey, tennis and cricket were all first organized and given rules in Britain. Rules are the essence of sport, and sportsmanship is the ability to practice a sport according to its rules, while also showing generosity to one's **opponent** and good temper in defeat. The high pressure of modern international sport makes these ideals difficult to keep, but they are at least highly valued in Britain and are certainly achieved there more commonly than among more excitable peoples. Moreover, sportsmanship as an ideal is applied to life in general and this is proved by the number of sporting terms used in ordinary speech. Everybody talks of "fair play" and "playing the game" or "playing fair." Borrowed from boxing, "straight from the shoulder" is used to describe a well-aimed strong criticism, and "below the belt" is used to describe an unfair one. One of the most **elementary** rules of life is "never hit a man when he's down." In other words, never take advantage of a person's misfortune. English schoolboys often show this sense of sportsmanship to a surprisingly high degree in their relations with each other.

After You Read

Knowledge Focus

1. **Work with your partner and share ideas with each other.**

   What would an Englishman or woman usually do in the following situations?

   ◇ An Englishman makes a journey to somewhere by train...

   ◇ An acquaintance asks an English lady's age...

   ◇ Someone pays compliments to an Englishman's skills in tennis...

   ◇ There's something quite funny happening in public and an Englishman happens to see it...

   ◇ An Englishman has just lost a tennis match...

2. **Write T if the statement is true and F if it is false.**

   _____ 1) A reserved person is one who is quite emotional, and tends to get excited easily.

   _____ 2) The British people are not noted for their generosity and hospitality.

   _____ 3) The Welsh are much less reserved than people of the South and the East.

   _____ 4) A sense of humor is an attitude to life rather than the mere ability to laugh at jokes.

   _____ 5) "Straight from the shoulder" and "below the belt" are sporting terms borrowed from rugby.

Language Focus

1. **Discuss the meanings of the bold-faced words in this text and work with a partner to fill in the blanks with a proper word or words.**

   1) While English people are, in general, *reserved*; the American people tend to be _____ .

   2) If a person is *reluctant* to communicate with others, he usually _____ to start a conversation.

   3) The hostess is very *hospitable*, and the guests are treated _____ .

   4) Whenever anyone mentions the word "*conceit*," the image of Mr. Darcy comes into mind, he was thought to be _____ .

   5) You'd better _____ those people who are sweet as honey to your face and as *malicious* as hell behind your back.

   6) If you seek help from a friend known for *generosity*, he is likely to _____ .

2. Fill in the blanks with the following expressions you have learned in the text.

be noted for	look down on	be keen on
due to	for a time	live up to
take advantage of		apply to

1) This rule cannot be _____ any case.

2) Students must _____ every opportunity to speak English.

3) Conceited people always _____ others.

4) _____ the police thought she might be guilty, but before long they eliminated her from their list of suspects.

5) This resort _____ its hot springs.

6) It's boring to stay at home all day long. I _____ outdoor sports.

7) His success is entirely _____ his hard work.

8) I hope I can _____ the expectations of my parents.

3. Fill in the blanks with the proper forms of words in the brackets.

1) A _____ (reserve) person is one who does not talk very much to strangers, does not show much emotion, and seldom gets excited.

2) This _____ (reluctant) to communicate with others is an unfortunate quality in some ways since it tends to give the impression of coldness.

3) It is true that the English (except perhaps those in the North) are not noted for their _____ (generous) and _____ (hospitable).

4) Closely related to English reserve is English _____ (modest).

5) To the English people, self-praise is felt to be _____ (polite).

6) The _____ (criticize) "He has no sense of humor" is very commonly heard in Britain, where humor is highly prized.

7) The typical Englishman secretly looks down on more _____ (excite) nations, and likes to think of himself as more _____ (rely) than they.

8) English schoolboys often show the sense of sportsmanship to a _____ (surprise) high degree in their relations with each other.

4. Proofreading and error correction.

The passage contains FIVE errors. Each indicated line contains a maximum of ONE error. In each case, only ONE word is involved. You should proofread the passage and correct it in the following way:

For a <u>wrong</u> word, underline the wrong word and write the correct one in the blank provided at the end of the line.

For a <u>missing</u> word, mark the position of the missing word with a " ∧ " sign and write the word you believe to be missing in the blank provided at the end of the line.

For an <u>unnecessary</u> word, cross the unnecessary word with a slash "/" and put the word in the blank provided at the end of the line.

The English are not usually giving to patriotic boasting—indeed, both patriotism and boasting are regarded as unseemly, the combination of these two sins is doubly distasteful. But there is one significant exception to this rule, and that is the patriotic pride we take with our sense of humour, particularly in our expert use of irony. The popular belief is that we have a better, more subtle, more highly developed sense of humour than any nation, and specifically that other nations are all tediously literal in their thinking and capable of understanding or appreciating irony.

1) _____

2) _____

3) _____

4) _____
5) _____

Comprehensive Work

1. **Study the following British sayings and try to use them to make dialogues.**

    1) A stitch in time saves nine.
    2) One man's meat is another man's poison.
    3) You can lead a horse to water, but you cannot make it drink.
    4) The grass is always greener on the other side.
    5) Don't cross your bridges before you come to them.
    6) The best advice is found on the pillow.
    7) Birds of a feather flock together.
    8) Don't look a gift horse in the mouth.

2. **Pair Work: Work with your partner and share ideas with each other.**

    Compare the English character with the American character. What are the similarities and differences?

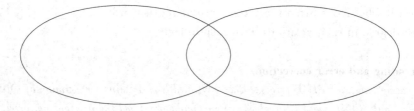

3. **Essay Writing**

    Write a passage of about 300 words, presenting your understanding of the following questions.

    ❖ Which aspect of the English character impresses you the most?
    ❖ Why?

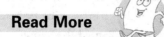

Read More

Text B   The English Character (II)

Read the following passage and finish the following exercises.

1) One can get the message from the first paragraph that it is _____ (likely/unlikely) to converse with the English in an intimate manner.

2) "*Silence is golden,*" "*Empty vessels make the most noise*" and "*You are not put on to this earth to enjoy yourself.*" From the sayings above, we can get the clue that the English parents want their children to be _____.

3) If there is one trait that absolutely singles out the English, it is their shared dislike for anyone or anything that "_____."

4) To the English, the proper way to behave in almost all situations is to display a languid _____ to almost everything. Even in affairs of the heart, it is considered unseemly to show one's feelings except _____.

5) The term is not exclusively a sporting one. It describes the sort of behaviour both on and off the playing field that characterises everything the English really respect. The term refers to "_____."

6) Whilst they may appear fearless and calm on the surface, deep down the English suffer from agonising self-doubt, feeling that in many areas of human activity they just cannot <u>cut the mustard</u>. The underlined expression means _____.

7) The English have a strong sense of history and they tend to fill their homes with _____.

8) The English are endlessly resourceful and inventive, but rarely _____ their inventions.

Stiff Upper Lip

The characteristic English pose involves keeping the head held high, the upper lip stiff and the best foot forward. In this position, conversation is difficult and intimacy of any kind almost impossible. This in itself is a clue to the English character.

Puritanism

Puritanism has always found in the English its most fertile breeding ground. For hundreds of years their children have been brainwashed with trite little sayings—"Silence is golden," "Empty vessels make the most noise" and, most telling, "You are not put on to this earth to enjoy yourself."

Small wonder that they end up, as adults, acting rather like the three wise monkeys and emotionally in traction.

But still the English defend their character and behaviour against all comers. Perhaps that is because Puritanism with its punishing work ethic assures them that their reward for all that restraint will come at a sort of school prize-giving ceremony in the world to come.

If it is the latter, they are forgetting that since God is also English—a firmly-held belief—any hedonism in the next world will probably be accompanied by mugs of bromide.

Nevertheless, the English continue to bask in this certainty to the general astonishment of the rest of mankind.

Moderation

If there is one trait that absolutely singles out the English, it is their shared dislike for anyone or anything that "goes too far."

Going too far, as the English see it, covers displaying an excess of emotion, getting drunk, discussing money in public or cracking off-colour jokes and then laughing at them noisily. Beyond the pale altogether is the man or woman who regales one with his or her titles or qualifications. The only acceptable place to air these is on an envelope.

To the English, the proper way to behave in almost all situations is to display a languid indifference to almost everything, though one may be seething underneath. Even in affairs of the heart, it is considered unseemly to show one's feelings except behind closed doors.

A Good Sport

If an English man or woman refers to you as "a good sport," you will know that you have really arrived. For to them, it is a qualification normally never awarded to a foreigner and by no means within the grasp of all the English.

The term is not exclusively a sporting one. It describes the sort of behaviour both on and off the playing field that characterises everything the English really respect. In all physical trials, the good sport will play without having been seen to practise too hard and will, ideally, win from innate superiority. He or she will then be dismissive of their victory and magnanimous towards the loser.

It goes without saying that the good sport will also be a good loser. There will be no arguing with umpires or outward signs of disappointment. On the contrary, a remark such as "The best man won!" tossed airily to all and sundry, and never through clenched teeth, is obligatory even in the face of crushing defeat.

This does not really fool anyone, for the English are fiercely competitive especially in matters of sporting. They would rather be crossed in love than beaten on the tennis courts, but to let it be seen would be going too far.

Self-Doubt

It is the apparent colossal self-confidence and moral certainty of the English that is paradoxically one of their greatest stumbling blocks. For both qualities are, to a certain extent, only illusions. Whilst they may appear fearless and calm on the surface, deep down the English suffer from agonising self-doubt, feeling that in many areas of human activity they just cannot cut the mustard.

All the time there were countries to be conquered and foreigners to be governed. The

English could sublimate all their clamouring uncertainty. The scent of success served as incense at the altar of their self-assurance.

But with the helter-skelter slide from Empire to Commonwealth and ever downwards, their doubts, like itches, have begun to plague them and it is considered bad form to scratch in public.

Sentiment

The English have a strong sense of history. Because their past was so infinitely more glamorous than their present, they cling to it tenaciously. Mix this love of bygone ages with an unrivalled sentimentality and you will have a heady mixture which can be sensed in every aspect of the English life.

Antique shops clutter up every town and village. English homes are filled with old things not only because they please the eye but because there is a feeling that anything that has stood the test of time must be better than its modern counterpart.

The English generally distrust the new-fangled or modern. Shininess is vulgar and the patina of age lends respectability. Thus they cling on to old furniture, old carpets, old chipped china, old kitchen gadgets and garden implements long after common sense dictates that they should be replaced.

"If it was good enough for my grandfather/grandmother, it's good enough for me!" The English cry goes up and each new invasion from the future is greeted with the indignant question: "What was wrong with the old one?" And as far as the English are concerned, there is no answer to that.

Inventiveness

The English are endlessly resourceful and inventive, but rarely profit from their inventions. The inventor in his garden shed turning out gadgets and widgets tends to be almost exclusively male, lacking the more practical female genes in any great numbers.

Often perceiving needs in daily life which have gone unobserved by the rest of his compatriots, he will beaver away 24 hours a day creating such indispensable items as the perfect egg boiler or the self-creasing trouser.

Occasionally, though, he will come up with something with real promise like the hovercraft which will then be ignored by his countrymen and taken up by foreigners.

Text C   The Understatement Rule

By Kate Fox

Read the following passage and then finish the exercises.

1) The understatement rule is a close cousin of the Importance of Not Being Earnest rule, the "Oh, come off it" rule and the various reserve and modesty rules that govern our

everyday social interactions. The underlined part means, _____.

2) Understatement is an exclusively English form of humor. The statement is _____ (True / False).

3) The English are rightly renowned for their use of understatement, because _____.

    a. they invented it   b. they practice it a lot   c. they do it better

4) Respond to the following occasions in the English understatement manner:

    a. a sight of breathtaking beauty _____

    b. an outstanding achievement _____

    c. an act of abominable cruelty _____

    d. an unforgivably stupid misjudgement _____.

5) Why do most foreigners find the English understatement hard to get?

I'm putting this as a sub-heading under irony, because understatement is a form of irony, rather than a distinct and separate type of humour. It is also a very English kind of irony—the understatement rule is a close cousin of the Importance of Not Being Earnest rule, the "Oh, come off it" rule and the various reserve and modesty rules that govern our everyday social interactions. Understatement is by no means an exclusively English form of humour, of course: again, we are talking about quantity rather than quality. George Mikes said that the understatement "is not just a speciality of the English sense of humour; it is a way of life." The English are rightly renowned for their use of understatement, not because we invented it or because we do it better than anyone else, but because we do it so much. (Well, maybe we do do it a little bit better—if only because we get more practice at it.)

The reasons for our prolific understating are not hard to discover: our strict prohibitions on earnestness, gushing, emoting and boasting require almost constant use of understatement. Rather than risk exhibiting any hint of forbidden solemnity, unseemly emotion or excessive zeal, we go to the opposite extreme and feign dry, deadpan indifference. The understatement rule means that a debilitating and painful chronic illness must be described as "a bit of a nuisance"; a truly horrific experience is "well, not exactly what I would have chosen"; a sight of breathtaking beauty is "quite pretty"; an outstanding performance or achievement is "not bad"; an act of abominable cruelty is "not very friendly," and an unforgivably stupid misjudgement is "not very clever"; the Antarctic is "rather cold" and the Sahara "a bit too hot for my taste"; and any exceptionally delightful object, person or event, which in other cultures would warrant streams of superlatives, is pretty much covered by "nice," or, if we wish to express more ardent approval, "very nice."

Needless to say, the English understatement is another trait that many foreign visitors find utterly bewildering and infuriating (or, as we English would put it, "a bit confusing"). "I don't get it," said one exasperated informant. "Is it supposed to be funny? If it's supposed to be funny, why don't they laugh—or at least smile? Or something. How the hell are you supposed to know when 'not bad' means 'absolutely brilliant' and when it just means 'OK'? Is there some secret sign or something that they use? Why can't they just say what they mean?"

This is the problem with English humour. Much of it, including and perhaps especially the understatement, isn't actually very funny—or at least not obviously funny, not laugh-out-loud funny, and definitely not crossculturally funny. Even the English, who understand it, are not exactly riotously amused by the understatement. At best, a well-timed, well-turned understatement only raises a slight smirk. But then, this is surely the whole point of the understatement: it is amusing, but only in an understated way. It is humour, but it is a restrained, refined, subtle form of humour.

Even those foreigners who appreciate the English understatement, and find it amusing, still experience considerable difficulties when it comes to using it themselves. My father tells me about some desperately anglophile Italian friends of his, who were determined to be as English as possible—they spoke perfect English, wore English clothes, even developed a taste for English food. But they complained that they couldn't quite "do" the English understatement, and pressed him for instructions. On one occasion, one of them was describing, heatedly and at some length, a ghastly meal he had had at a local restaurant—the food was inedible, the place was disgustingly filthy, the service rude beyond belief, etc. "Oh," said my father, at the end of the tirade, "So, you wouldn't recommend it, then?" "You See?" cried his Italian friend. "That's it! How do you do that? How do you know to do that? How do you know when to do it?" "I don't know," said my father apologetically. "I can't explain. We just do it. It just comes naturally."

This is the other problem with the English understatement: it is a rule, but a rule in the fourth OED sense of "the normal or usual state of things"—we are not conscious of obeying it; it is somehow wired into our brains. We are not taught the use of the understatement, we learn it by osmosis. The understatement "comes naturally" because it is deeply ingrained in our culture, part of the English psyche.

The understatement is also difficult for foreigners to "get" because it is, in effect, an in-joke about our own unwritten rules of humour. When we describe, say, a horrendous, traumatic and painful experience as "not very pleasant," we are acknowledging the taboo on earnestness and the rules of irony, but at the same making fun of our ludicrously rigid obedience to these codes. We are exercising restraint, but in such an exaggerated manner that we are also (quietly) laughing at ourselves for doing so. We are parodying ourselves. Every understatement is a little private joke about Englishness.

Notes

Winston Churchill (1874—1965): He was a British politician known chiefly for his leadership of the United Kingdom during World War II. He served as Prime Minister of the United Kingdom from 1940 to 1945 and again from 1951 to 1955. A noted statesman and orator, Churchill was also an officer in the British Army, a historian, a Nobel Prize-winning writer, and an artist.

For Fun

Books to read

Around the World in Eighty Days by Jules Verne—Phileas Fogg bets half his fortune against other members of the Reform Club that he can travel around the world in 80 days or less.

The English National Character by Peter Mandler—a historian of modern Britain challenges long-held familiar stereotypes and proposes an entirely new perspective on what it means to think of oneself as being English.

Watching the English：*The Hidden Rules of English Behaviour* by Kate Fox—It's a fascinating and insightful book，but what really sets it apart is the informal style aimed squarely at the intelligent layman.

Movies to see

Notting Hill—The life of a simple bookshop owner changes when the most famous star in the world walks into his shop and buys a book...

Mr. Bean—Life is a difficult challenge for Mr. Bean，who has trouble completing even the simplest of tasks. Thankfully，his perseverance is usually rewarded，and he finds an ingenious way around the problem.

Unit 2
The Constitutional Monarchy

> Like all the best families, we have our share of eccentricities, of impetuous and wayward youngsters and of family disagreements.
>
> —Queen Elizabeth II

Unit Goals

● To understand the role of the monarchy in the U.K.
● To get to know the constitutional monarchy system in the U.K.
● To develop critical thinking and intercultural communication skills
● To learn useful words and expressions concerning the constitutional monarchy system in the U.K. and improve English language skills

Before You Read

Can you recognize the following figures? Talk with your partner about what you know about them.

Start to Read

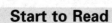

Text A   **The Constitutional Monarchy**

1 The term **Constitutional Monarchy** may seem surprising in view of the great **affection** which the British have for Queen Elizabeth(1926—2022), the

great ceremonies connected with her, the great state functions over which she **presided**, the oaths of loyalty made to her by Parliament, and the many great decisions made in her name and requiring her **authority**. It was the Queen who approved the **appointment** of ministers and the formation of a cabinet; it was the Queen who summoned Parliament and who introduced the new session with a speech from the Throne in which she summarized the government's program; it was the Queen who gave her **assent** to Bills before they became law, who concluded treaties and declared war, who made appointments to all offices of State and Church, who **dismissed** Parliament when the government had been defeated or had reached the end of its term, and who chose a new Prime Minister. Indeed, she was informed and **consulted** on every aspect of national life.

2 And yet it remains true that she had no power. For in practice, she acted only on the advice of her ministers, and must be completely **impartial**. The Queen never refused her assent, because she knew this would be **unconstitutional**. In any case, she had no means of enforcing her will.

3 However, most British people regard the Monarchy as a long-established tradition, which, with all its color and **pageantry** and with all the feelings of personal respect which it inspires, they would be most unwilling to lose. The British love tradition; the Queen **represents** much that is traditional. New traditions are soon established to fit into modern developments; for example, the Queen was seen on television every year, broadcasting a Christmas message to the nation. She enjoyed country life and sports, and she was interested in horseracing, pursuits much loved by many ordinary Britons. The Queen set an example of good family life.

4 More than this, the Monarch is the only unchangeable symbol of Britain itself. Politicians come and go according to elections won or lost, and at any given moment every politician always **determines** opponents among those who do not belong to his own party. But the Monarch is always there, above party quarrels, representing the nation as a whole, and lending dignity and significance to all things done in her name.

5 The Queen worked extremely hard, reading state papers, signing documents, receiving ambassadors and important visitors from abroad. She saw the Prime Minister once a week to discuss affairs of state. Any criticism of the monarchy usually **concerns** the amount of money Parliament provides for the Royal Family. But the British enjoy **ceremonial**. They are good at organizing ceremonies which are full of drama and color. The Queen was the center of many of them.

6 Relations between the Monarch, or **Sovereign**, and the Prime Minister are a private matter, and must depend very much on the **personality** of each. But at least one Prime Minister has said that the **necessity** of taking all cabinet decisions to the Sovereign, even though the Sovereign could do nothing to **alter** them, sometimes has a definite and **beneficial** influence on the kind of decisions taken.

7 The British Monarchy is the supreme **illustration** of the way British institutions develop. Violent **upheavals** are rare. Instead, the existing system is slowly **modified** to suit fresh conditions, until in the end the impossible is achieved—a completely new system which still looks exactly like the old. And the pride of the British is that although it is **illogical**, it works.

After You Read

Knowledge Focus

1. **What were the Queen's state functions? Complete the following sentences.**
   1) The Queen approved the appointment of _____ and the formation of a _____.
   2) The Queen summoned _____ and introduced the new _____ with a speech from the Throne in which she summarized _____.
   3) The Queen gave her assent to _____ before they became law.
   4) The Queen concluded _____ and declared war, made appointments to all offices of _____, dismissed Parliament when the government had been _____ or had reached _____, and chose a new _____.
   5) The Queen was _____ and _____ on every aspect of national life.
   6) The Queen signed documents and received _____ and important visitors from abroad.

2. Write T if the statement is true and F if it is false.

1) The Monarch represents the interest of the governing party. (　)

2) The Monarch has no real power. In practice，the Monarch acts only on the advice of the Prime Minister. (　)

3) It is constitutional for the Monarch to refuse her assent. (　)

4) The Monarch sees the Prime Minister once a month to discuss affairs of state. (　)

5) Sometimes the Sovereign has a definite and beneficial influence on the cabinet decisions taken. (　)

Language Focus

1. Fill in the blanks with a proper word in proper form.

preside	summon	assent	dismiss	consult
beneficial	modify	concern	determine	represent

1) The exam results could _____ your career.

2) Fresh air is _____ to our health.

3) Some people believe that the Fates _____ over man's destiny.

4) She _____ her fellow-workers at the union meeting.

5) The new law has received the royal _____.

6) I have _____ a number of law books in the British Museum.

7) These problems _____ all of us and we should solve them as soon as possible.

8) He'll have to _____ his views if he wants to be elected.

9) The boss threatened to _____ him from his job, but it's all a bluff.

10) The shareholders were _____ to a general meeting.

2. Fill in the blanks with the following expressions you have learned in the text.

in view of	full of drama	in one's name
fit into	more than	

1) Your plan is great，but it does not _____ my schedule.

2) She wishes to be treated as nothing _____ a common girl.

3) _____ our long-standing relationship，we agree to allow you a discount.

4) I don't expect to live a life _____, and I just want to live every day peacefully.

5) The Parliament made many great decisions _____ the Queen's _____.

3. Fill in the blanks with the proper form of the words in the brackets.

1) It seems _____ (logical) to change the timetable so often.

2) To give a definition of a word is more difficult than to give an _____ (illustrate) of its use.

3) His _____ (person) is clearly reflected in his writing.

4) _____ (Necessary) is the mother of invention.

5) Calcium is _____ (benefit) to our bones.

6) Her career culminated in her _____ (appoint) as director.

7) People in the city held the _____ (partial) judge in high regard.

8) He's so susceptible that she easily gained his _____ (affect).

4. Proofreading and error correction.

The passage contains FIVE errors. Each indicated line contains a maximum of ONE error. In each case, only ONE word is involved.

In recent years, the monarchy is all but fallen into disrepute in Britain. It was the butt of sophisticated humour on television programmes and became the subject of much tabloid treatment ridiculed the affairs of Prince Charles, Prince Andrew and their wives. To compound so adverse publicity, Buckingham Palace has proved inept at handling the British media. Opponents of the Palace used to the newspapers against them, publishing for example Prince Charles's conversations with his long-term lover Mrs Camilla Parker-Bowles. Broadcasts of this and other gaffes turned the royals into beleaguered, if not endangered, institution.	1) _____ 2) _____ 3) _____ 4) _____ 5) _____

Comprehensive Work

1. Group Work: Discuss the following topic in groups of four. Summarize the views of your group and present them to class orally.

Since the monarchy's job is primarily symbolic, do you think there's the necessity for the monarchy to exist? Why do you think the Britons still keep the monarchy in modern time?

2. Essay Writing

Write a passage of about 300 words, presenting your understanding of the following questions.

❖ What do you think of the royal family in the U.K.?

❖ What roles do you think the royal family should play?

Read More

Text B   The Role of the Monarchy Today

Read the following passage and decide whether the following statements are true or false. Write T if the statement is true and F if it is false.

1) The Monarch represents the interest of the government. _____

2) Much of the financial support for the Royal family comes from the taxpayer. _____

3) The Monarch is the "supreme governor" of the Church of England. _____

4) Every Thursday the Prime Minister attends the Monarch privately at Buckingham Palace. _____

5) The real power of monarchy has gradually been reduced and today the Monarch acts solely on the advice of the ministers. _____

6) The Monarch reigns but does not rule. _____

The role of the monarchy today is primarily to symbolize the tradition and unity of the British state. Obviously the Prime Minister and governing party at any given time will only represent the part of the population that voted in their favour. However, being non-political, the Monarch belongs to everybody. Under the terms of the constitution, other monarchic roles are as follows: head of the executive, an integral part of the legislature, head of the judiciary, commander-in-chief of the armed forces and "supreme governor" of the Church of England.

In a 1988 poll, most Britons felt the Queen's most important job was to represent Britain at home and abroad; her second most important job was to set standards of good citizenship and family life. The royal family occupies the position of First Family and is expected to set an example in both public and private life. With the growth of the modern media industry—press, radio, television—the official and unofficial lives of royalty are becoming increasingly exposed. While the Queen indeed led an exemplary life, her children have been criticized for their poor behavior.

While the Monarch is independently wealthy, much of the financial support for the Royal family comes from the taxpayer, supposedly in recognizance of the fact that the royal family fulfills its role on behalf of the British people. This has led to great controversy in recent years.

A more general criticism about the monarchy and the debate came to a head in November 1992 when a fire did a great deal of damage to Windsor Castle. The government immediately offered 50 million pounds' worth of taxpayer's money to pay for repairs. The electorate was very angry: Britain was in a recession and the basic things like hospitals and schools had been forced to cut their services because public money was so scarce. They thought it was very unfair that the Queen, who was incredibly wealthy and did not have to pay taxes herself, should not have to pay for at least part of the repairs. The taxpayer was already paying for the running costs of Buckingham Palace, Windsor Castle, three other palaces, a royal yacht, a royal train and a royal plane. As a result of the controversy, the Queen offered to start paying taxes and to accept less public money to support her family. She also began to open Buckingham Palace to tourists in the summer months in order to raise money to pay for repairs. Her willingness to give in to popular demands once again endeared her to her subjects, although her children still remain quite unpopular.

A less well-known role of the Monarch, which is nevertheless very important to British politics, is that of a confidant to the Prime Minister. Every Tuesday the Prime Minister attends the Monarch privately at Buckingham Palace. Interestingly, it is said that the Queen got on much better with Labour Prime Ministers than with Conservative Prime Ministers.

In practice, over the centuries, the real power of monarchy has gradually been reduced and today the Monarch acts solely on the advice of the ministers. The Monarch reigns but does not rule. The principal role is symbolic: the Monarch must represent the nation's present-day hopes and ideals as well as its historic past.

Text C   Charles III's First National Television Address

Read the following passage and finish the following exercises.

1) In his first National Television Address Charles III paid tribute to _____.
2) Which of the following statements is NOT true? _____
    A. Queen Elizabeth II served her people for more than 70 years.
    B. Queen Elizabeth II came to the throne before WWII.
    C. The monarch is also responsible for the Church of England.
3) Now William succeeds Charles III and assumes the titles of Duke of _____ and Prince of _____.
4) Match the names with the titles

Charles	Tywysog Cymru
Camilla	Princess of Wales
Catherine	Queen Consort
William	The King

I speak to you today with feelings of profound sorrow. Throughout her life, Her Majesty the Queen—my beloved mother—was an inspiration and example to me and to all my family, and we owe her the most heartfelt debt any family could owe to their mother, for her love, affection, guidance, understanding and example.

Queen Elizabeth was a life well lived, a promise with destiny kept, and she's mourned most deeply in her passing. That promise of lifelong service I renew to all today. Alongside the personal grief that all my family are feeling, we also share with so many of you in the United Kingdom, in all the countries where the Queen was Head ofState, in the Commonwealth and across the world, a deep sense of gratitude for the more than 70 years in which my mother, as Queen, served the people of so many nations.

In 1947, on her 21st birthday, she pledged in a broadcast from Cape Town to the Commonwealth to devote her life, whether it be short or long, to the service of her peoples. That was more than a promise: it was a profound personal commitment which defined her whole life. She made sacrifices for duty. Her dedication and devotion as sovereign never wavered, through times of change and progress, through times of joy and celebration, and through times of sadness and loss. In her life of service, we saw that abiding love of tradition, together with that fearless embrace of progress, which makes us great as Nations. The affection, admiration and respect she inspired became the hallmark in her reign. And, as every member of my family can testify, she combined these qualities with warmth, humour and an unerring ability always to see the best in people. I pay tribute to my mother's memory, and I honor her life of service. I know that her death brings great sadness to so many of you and I share that sense of loss, beyond measure, with you all.

When the Queen came to the throne, Britain and the world were still coping with the privations and aftermath of the Second World War, and still living by the conventions of earlier times. In the course of the last 70 years, we have seen our society become one of many cultures and many faiths. The institutions of the State have changed in turn. But, through all changes and challenges, our nation and the wider family of realms—of whose talents, traditions and achievements I am so inexpressively proud—have prospered and flourished. Our values have remained, and must remain, constant. The role and the duties of Monarchy also remain, as does the Sovereign' sparticular relationship and responsibility towards the Church of England—the Church in which my own faith is so deeply rooted. In that faith, and the values it inspires, I have been brought up to cherish a sense of duty to others, and to hold in the greatest respect the precious traditions, freedoms and responsibilities of our unique history and our system of parliamentary government.

As the Queen herself did with such unswerving devotion, I too now solemnly pledged myself, throughout the remaining time God grants me, to uphold the Constitutional principles at the heart of our nation. And wherever you may live in the United Kingdom, or in the Realms and territories across the world, and whatever may be your background or beliefs, I shallendeavour to serve you with loyalty, respect and love, as I have throughout my life. My life will of course change as I take up my new responsibilities. It will no longer be possible for me to give so much of my time and energies to the charities and issues for which I care so deeply. But I know this important work will go on in their trusted hands of others. This is also a time of change from my family. I count on the loving help of my darling wife Camilla. In recognition of her own loyal public service since our marriage 17 years ago, she becomes my Queen Consort. I know she will bring to the demands of her new role the steadfast devotion to duty on which I have come to rely so much. As my heir, William now assumes the Scottish titles which have meant so much to me. He succeeds me as Duke of Cornwall and takes on the responsibilities for the Duchy of Cornwall which I have undertaken for more than five decades. Today, I am proud to create him Prince of Wales, Tywysog Cymru, the country whose title I have been so greatly privileged to bear during so much of my life and duty. With Catherine beside him, our new Prince and Princess of Wales will, I know, continue to inspire and lead our national conversations, helping to bring the marginal to the centre ground where vital help can be given. I want also to express my love to Harry and Meghan, as they continue to build their lives overseas.

In a little over a week's time, we will come together as a nation, as a Commonwealth and indeed a global community, to lay my beloved mother to rest. In our sorrow, let us remember and draw strength from the light of her example. On behalf of all my family, I can only offer the most sincere and heartfelt thanks for your condolences and support. They mean more to me than I can ever possibly express. And to my darling Mama, as you begin your last great journey to join my dear late Papa, I want simply to say this: thank you. Thank you for your love and devotion to our family and to the family of nations you have served so diligently all these years. May "flights of Angels sing thee to thy rest."

Text D   Diana, the People's Princess

Read the following passage and finish the following exercises.

1) Matching

A. embcd	a. violent or confused movement
B. on end	b. to get rid of
C. transform	c. to become fixed firmly
D. turmoil	d. a public sale of goods or property
E. auction	e. not diminishing in determination, effort, etc
F. discard	f. continuously
G. unrelenting	g. to change the form of

2) Arrange the following events in chronological order and mark the events with numbers.

_____ Diana followed her sisters to Westheath School in Kent.

_____ The Spencers moved to Parkhouse on the Sundream Estate.

_____ Diana was offered a post in a London kindergarten.

_____ Diana and Price Charles announced their engagement.

_____ Diana died in a car accident in Paris.

_____ Princess Diana and Prince Charles divorced from each other.

_____ Diana's parents separated from each other.

Diana Spencer was born on July 1st, 1961. Her family, the Spencers of Atthorp had been wealthy landowners since the 16th century, whose roots were embedded deep in English history. Her family has lived on the edge of the royal circle. The marriage of her parents has been attended by the Queen. Her father, Earl Spencer, was an equerry to King George VI. These ties paved the way for the Spencers to move to Parkhouse on the Sundream Estate. During these early years, the young Diana often saw her royal neighbours. She played with royalty, but it would not prepare her for what was to come. At the age of six, her parents separated, a moment she would never forget.

In 1973, Diana followed her sisters to Westheath School in Kent. The routine of a country house style boarding school was intended to give her life the stability that no longer existed at home. Although she was popular, she lacked confidence. At school, teachers would recall her practicing dives for hours on end. Academically, however, she was less successful.

At Westheath, she had discovered her love of working with children. In 1979, after a brief period at a Swiss finishing school, she was offered a post in a London kindergarten.

Through family connection, she had been introduced to Prince Charles. In 1981, they announced their engagement. She married Prince Charles, a man twelve years her senior. She transformed into Diana, the Princess of Wales, a new and glamorous addition to Britain's stuffy Royal Family, and an instant celebrity. Within three years, she had given birth to two sons, Prince William and Prince Harry. She was a devoted mother.

The fairy tale seemed complete, but there was a sadness few guessed at. Diana and Charles were not the perfect match. They seemed unable to share common tastes, and were soon rarely seemed together. In 1997, Princess Diana and Prince Charles were finally divorced, and it was the nightmare she had promised herself would never happen. She had lost her title "Her Royal Highness," but she was a famous woman in search of her role in public life.

She made trips to Bosnia and Angola, drawing attention to the human misery caused by mines left behind when conflicts were over. She campaigned for governments to ban the production, export and stock piling and use of anti-personal mines.

She had visited Mother Teresa who was in poor health. After the years of turmoil, it seemed Diana was reestablishing herself as a confident public figure, lending her reputation to the sisters of mercy.

She auctioned off 79 dresses and ball gowns that had been featured on so many front covers. It symbolized a discarding of the past. Her favorite charities included those for cancer and AIDS sufferers. When she was in Paris in 1997, she was pursued by modern day bounty hunters and it led to tragedy in a Paris underpass—she died at the age of 36.

Diana died as she had lived for 19 years in the unrelenting gaze of the publicity. With her youthful vitality, she became the human face of an ancient institution, changing forever the public perception of monarchy.

On the Death of Princess Diana
by Her Majesty Queen Elizabeth II, Queen of the United Kingdom

The Queen spoke to the nation live at 6:00 p.m. on Friday, 5 September, from the Chinese Dining Room at Buckingham Palace, 1997.

Since last Sunday's dreadful news we have seen, throughout Britain and around the world, an overwhelming expression of sadness at Diana's death.

We have all been trying in our different ways to cope. It is not easy to express a sense of loss, since the initial shock is often succeeded by a mixture of other feelings: disbelief, incomprehension, anger—and concern for those who remain.

We have all felt those emotions in these last few days. So what I say to you now, as your queen and as a grandmother, I say from my heart.

First, I want to pay tribute to Diana myself. She was an exceptional and gifted human being. In good times and bad, she never lost her capacity to smile and laugh, nor to inspire others with her warmth and kindness.

I admired and respected her—for her energy and commitment to others, and especially for her devotion to her two boys.

This week at Balmoral, we have all been trying to help William and Harry come to terms with the devastating loss that they and the rest of us have suffered.

No one who knew Diana will ever forget her. Millions of others who never met her, but felt they knew her, will remember her.

I for one believe that there are lessons to be drawn from her life and from the extraordinary and moving reaction to her death.

I share in your determination to cherish her memory.

This is also an opportunity for me, on behalf of my family, and especially Prince Charles and William and Harry, to thank all of you who have brought flowers, sent messages, and paid your respects in so many ways to a remarkable person.

These acts of kindness have been a huge source of help and comfort.

Our thoughts are also with Diana's family and the families of those who died with her. I know that they too have drawn strength from what has happened since last weekend, as they seek to heal their sorrow and then to face the future without a loved one.

I hope that tomorrow we can all, wherever we are, join in expressing our grief at Diana's loss, and gratitude for her all-too-short life.

It is a chance to show to the whole world the British nation united in grief and respect.

May those who died rest in peace and may we, each and every one of us, thank God for someone who made many, many people happy.

Know More

Elizabeth II (1926—2022)

Elizabeth II became Queen of the United Kingdom of Great Britain and Northern Ireland in 1952.

Elizabeth was born on 21 April 1926 in London, the first child of Albert, Duke of York, and his wife, formerly Lady Elizabeth Bowes-Lyon. She initially had little prospect of succeeding to the throne until her uncle, Edward VIII, abdicated in December 1936. Her

father then became George VI and she became heir.

The Queen's official title in the United Kingdom is:

"*Elizabeth the Second, by the Grace of God of the United Kingdom of Great Britain and Northern Ireland and of Her Other Realms and Territories Queen, Head of the Commonwealth, Defender of the Faith.*"

Notes

1. **King George VI** (1895—1952): He was King of the United Kingdom and the British Dominions from 11 December 1936 until his death. He was the last Emperor of India until 1947 and the last King of Ireland until 1949. George VI ascended the throne, when his brother Edward VIII, abdicated to marry a twice-divorced American woman. George VI married Lady Elizabeth Bowes-Lyon in 1923, and they had two daughters, Elizabeth, who succeeded him as Queen Elizabeth II, and Margaret.

2. **Mother Teresa** (1910—1997): She was an Albanian Roman Catholic nun with Indian citizenship who founded the Missionaries of Charity in Kolkata (Calcutta), India in 1950. For over 45 years, she ministered to the poor, sick, orphaned, and dying, while guiding the Missionaries of Charity's expansion, first throughout India and then in other countries.

For Fun

Movies to see

The Queen—After the death of Princess Diana, Queen Elizabeth II struggles with her reaction to a sequence of events nobody could have predicted.

The Prince and Me—A fairy tale love-story about a common girl who falls in love with a Danish Prince who refused to follow the traditions of his parents and has come to the U.S. to quench his thirst for rebellion.

Song to enjoy

Elton John, *Candle in the Wind*—Goodbye England's Rose, may you ever grow in our hearts, you were the grace that placed itself where lives were torn apart...

Unit 3
The British Parliament

> We make a living by what we get, but we make a life by what we give.
>
> —Sir Winston Churchill

Unit Goals

● To understand the role of Parliament in the U.K.
● To get some information about the political parties in the U.K.
● To develop critical thinking and intercultural communication skills
● To learn useful words and expressions concerning the Parliamentary democracy in the U.K. and improve English language skills

Before You Read

1. Review what you have learned: the government system of the U.S.

Branch	People	Responsibilities
Executive	( ) Cabinet	( )
( )	Congress 100 ( ) 435 ( )	make laws
( )	Supreme Court ( )	( )

2. Talk with your partner and share ideas with each other.
   How much do you know about the U.K. government system? What are the major differences between the U.K. government system and the U.S. government system?

25

Start to Read

Text A **The British Government Today**

1 The British government today is deeply influenced by its long past. Britain is both a **parliamentary democracy** and a **constitutional monarchy**. While the official head of state is the Monarch, monarchic powers are largely traditional and symbolic. The government at national and local levels is elected by people and governs according to British constitutional principles.

The Constitution

2 British governance today is based upon the terms and conditions of the constitution. Israel and Britain are the only two countries without written constitutions of the sort which most countries have, instead of having one particular document which lists out the basic principles of how a country should be governed, the foundations of the British state are laid out in **statute laws**, that is, laws passed by Parliament; the **common laws**, which are laws which have been established through common practice in the courts, not because Parliament has written them; and **conventions**, which are rules and practices which do not exist legally, but are **nevertheless** regarded as **vital** to the workings of government.

Parliament

3 Parliament has a number of different functions. First and foremost, it passes laws. Another important function is that it provides the means of carrying on the work of government by voting for **taxation**. Its other roles are to **scrutinize** government policy, **administration** and **expenditure** and to debate the major issues of the day.

4 Strictly speaking, Parliament today consists of the Monarch, the House of Lords and the House of Commons. These three **institutions** must all agree to pass any given legislation.

5 However, most everyday references to Parliament refer to the workings of the Lords and the Commons, with the Monarch regarded as a separate institution. This is because even though the Monarch must **consent** to pass a law, this consent is given as a matter of course.

6 Below the Monarch is the House of Lords. It consists of the Lords Spiritual, who are the Archbishops and most **prominent** bishops of the Church of England; and the Lords Temporal, which refers to everyone else. Lords, usually called peers, are not elected and are not considered to represent anyone besides themselves. They sit in the Lords either because they have **inherit**ed the seat from their **forefathers** or because they have been appointed by the sovereign, at the suggestion of the Prime Minister. These latter are called **life peers**.

7 Because peers are appointed or given the right by their birth into a particular family, in Parliament they speak and vote as individuals, not as representatives of the greater interests of the country—although of course **civic-minded** peers do try to serve their country rather than their own interests. Unlike those who serve in the House of Commons, they do not receive salaries and many do not attend Parliament at all. Although the House of Lords is **restricted** in its powers, it can still serve a useful purpose. Its debating is often of a very high standard, and it often puts forward useful amendments which are later accepted by the Commons. Some bills of a **noncontroversial** nature are actually introduced in the House of Lords, this **relieving** the Commons of some of its work.

8 The House of Commons is a democratically elected body consisting of about 650 members called Members of Parliament (MPs). Each member is elected by and represents an **electoral** district of Britain known as a **constituency**. The great majority of MPs represent English constituencies and only a few of them represent Scotland, Welsh and Northern Ireland, **respectively**. MPs are only allowed to sit for the lifetime of the Parliament, that is, the length of time between **General Elections** when a new set of MPs is elected. Unlike the Lords, MPs receive a salary which is about the same pay as an average middle class professional such as a doctor or an accountant would earn and it is thought that MPs will thus be able to **identify** with the "typical" voter they represent.

9 Most MPs belong to political parties—Labour, the Conservatives and the Liberal Democrats are the major ones. The Prime Minister is of course the leader of the political party which wins the most seats in a general election. His or her Cabinet nowadays consists of usually around 20 MPs in the governing party who are chosen by the Prime Minister to become government ministers in the Cabinet. The Cabinet carries out the functions of policy-making, the coordination of government

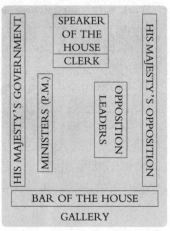

departments and the supreme control of government. The House of Commons is the real center of British political life.

After You Read

Knowledge Focus

1. Fill in this graphic organizer with information about how the U. K. government is organized.

The Parliament	People	Responsibility on Law-Making
The Monarch	(　　)	consent to pass laws
House of (　　)	Lords Spiritual Lords (　　)	review laws
House of (　　)	MPs	(　　)

2. Write T if the statement is true and F if it is false.
   1) Like any other country, the U. K. also has a written constitution. _____
   2) Statute laws are laws which have been established through common practice in the courts. _____
   3) Strictly speaking, Parliament today consists of the King, the House of Lords and the House of Commons. _____
   4) Life peers are lords who have inherited the seat from their forefathers. _____
   5) The Prime Minister is the leader of the governing political party. _____
   6) The House of Commons is the real center of British political life. _____

Language Focus

1. Work with your partner and explain the meanings of the following terms in your own words.
   1) parliamentary democracy

   _____

   2) constitutional monarchy

   _____

   3) statute laws

   _____

   4) life peers

   _____

5) constituency

_____

6) MPs

_____

2. **Fill in the blanks with the following words you have learned in the text.**

vital	forefather	inherit	consent
prominent	identify	nevertheless	restrict
relieve	respectively		

1) The experiment failed. It was, _____, worth making.

2) The house is in a _____ position on the village green.

3) This matter is of _____ importance to us.

4) I found it hard to _____ with any of the characters in the film.

5) One of his _____ was an early settler in America.

6) My husband and I got pay rises by 8% and 10% _____.

7) She has _____ all her mother's beauty.

8) Her father will never give his _____ to our marriage.

9) The route was designed to _____ traffic congestion.

10) The government will introduce legislation to _____ the sale of firearms.

3. **Fill in the blanks with the following expressions you have learned in the text.**

lay out	first and foremost	put forward
refer to	as a matter of course	consist of
instead of	carry out	

1) I told him he had won the first prize; he took it _____.

2) —How do you like the house?

—I love it. It is _____ sensibly.

3) We should try all means to help those refugees; _____ they need food.

4) They swore an oath to _____ their duties faithfully.

5) How many players does a baseball team _____?

6) There is a growing tendency for people to work at home _____ in offices.

7) In his speech, he didn't _____ the problem at all.

8) These foreigners have _____ a proposal for a joint venture.

4. **Proofreading and error correction.**

The passage contains FIVE errors. Each indicated line contains a maximum of ONE error. In each case, only ONE word is involved.

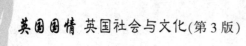
The British parliament has its origins in the thirteenth-century baronial councils. It is now bicameral chamber includes the monarch or the monarch's representative. Currently its full name is "The King in Parliament," and it is a sovereign body that cover England, Wales, Scotland (since 1707) and Northern Ireland (since 1922). Under a variety of treaty, some of its powers have been ceded to the European Union. Some of its prerogatives have also been ceded through international treaties as the United Nations Declaration on Human Rights.	1) _____ 2) _____ 3) _____ 4) _____ 5) _____

Comprehensive Work

1. **Discuss the following topic in groups of four. Summarize the views of your group and present them to class orally.**

    Compare the U.S. government system with the U.K. government system. Which system do you think can work better?

    What are the advantages and disadvantages of each system?

Potential or Possible Advantages	Potential or Possible Disadvantages

2. **Essay Writing**

    Write a passage of about 300 words, presenting your understanding of the following questions.

    ❖ Does the statement "Government is a necessary evil" make any sense to you?

    ❖ How do you undertand the statement?

Read More

Text B   Political Parties in the U.K.

1. **Read the following passage and finish the following exercises.**

    1) The two major parties in the U.K. are the _____ party and the _____ party.

    2) The _____ party is a socialist party and it believes a society should be relatively equal in economic terms, and that part of the role of government is to act as a "redistributive" agent, and it is known as a party of high _____ levels.

    3) From 1979 to 1997, the Conservative party won 4 elections in a row and was in

power for a long period. The underlined expression means _____.

4) Basically, the _____ party is seen as the party of the individual, and it receives a lot of their party funding from big companies.

2. Talk with your partner on the following question.

Which party beliefs do you think are more reasonable? Why?

The Labour party is comparatively a new party, created by the growing trade union movement at the end of the nineteenth century. It quickly replaced the Liberal party as one of the two biggest parties (nineteenth century politics had essentially been a competition between the Liberals and the Conservatives). Labour is a socialist party. They believe a society should be relatively equal in economic terms, and that part of the role of government is to act as a "redistributive" agent: transferring wealth from the richer to poorer by means of taxing the richer part of society and providing support to the poorer part of society. Besides this redistributive role, they see the government as the right body to provide a range of public services available to all, such as health, education and public transport.

The Labour government that came to power in 1945 had a major effect on British society: setting up the National Health Service to provide high quality health care for all, free, "from cradle to grave"; providing a range of welfare payments to replace or supplement wages in case of unemployment, sickness, poverty, etc.; and, most controversially, it "nationalised" a wide range of industries, making the U. K. into a mixed economy with both private enterprises and a large state-owned sector. All this government activity required money, so the Labour party became known as a party of high taxation levels.

The Conservative party is the party that stay long in power. In the post-1945 period, the party of government changed fairly frequently, as Labour government was replaced by Conservative and vice versa. From 1979 to 1997, the Conservative party won 4 elections in a row and was in power for a long period. Basically, the Conservatives are seen as the party of the individual, protecting the individual's right to acquire wealth and to spend it the way they choose, and so favouring economic policies which businessmen prefer, such as low taxes. They receive a lot of their party funding from big companies.

But in the past, this economic policy was coupled with a "fatherly" sense of obligation to the less fortunate in society, which meant that even though the "Big" government which Labour set up in the post-1945 era was against their principles, they did not dismantle it when they were in power. Thus the difference between the Labour party and the Conservative party is one of degree, not an absolute.

 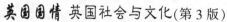

Text C   Margaret Thatcher

Read the following passage and arrange the following events in chronological order and mark the events with numbers.

_____ Thatcher became Conservative member of parliament for Finchley in north London.

_____ Thatcher became Prime Minister.

_____ Thatcher left the House of Commons for the House of Lords as Baroness Thatcher of Kesteven.

_____ Thatcher went to Oxford University and then became a research chemist.

_____ Thatcher served in a number of positions in Edward Heath's shadow cabinet.

_____ Thatcher married a wealthy businessman, Denis Thatcher.

_____ Thatcher narrowly escaped death when the IRA planted a bomb at the Conservative party conference in Brighton.

_____ Thatcher agreed to resign and was succeeded as party leader and Prime Minister by John Major.

Margaret Thatcher (1925—2013) was Britain's first female Prime Minister and served three consecutive terms in office. She is one of the dominant political figures of the 20th century Britain, and Thatcherism continues to have a huge influence.

Margaret Hilda Roberts was born on 13 October 1925 in Grantham, Lincolnshire, the daughter of a grocer. She went to Oxford University and then became a research chemist, retraining to become a barrister in 1954. In 1951, she married a wealthy businessman, Denis Thatcher, with whom she had two children.

Thatcher became Conservative member of parliament for Finchley in north London in 1959, serving as its MP until 1992. Her first parliamentary post was junior minister for pensions in Harold Macmillan's government. From 1964 to 1970, when Labour were in power, she served in a number of positions in Edward Heath's shadow cabinet. Heath became Prime Minister in 1970 and Thatcher was appointed secretary for education.

After the Conservatives were defeated in 1974, Thatcher challenged Heath for the leadership of the party and, to the surprise of many, won. In the 1979 general election, the Conservatives came to power and Thatcher became Prime Minister.

An advocate of privatisation of state-owned industries and utilities, reform of the trade unions, the lowering of taxes and reduced social expenditure across the board, Thatcher succeeded in reducing inflation, but unemployment dramatically increased.

Victory in the Falklands War in 1982 and a divided opposition helped Thatcher win a landslide victory in the 1983 general election. In 1984, she narrowly escaped death when the IRA planted a bomb at the Conservative party conference in Brighton.

In foreign affairs, Thatcher cultivated a close political and personal relationship with U. S. president Ronald Reagan, based on a common mistrust of communism, combined with free-market economic ideology. Thatcher was nicknamed the "Iron Lady" by the Soviets. She warmly welcomed the rise of reformist Soviet leader Mikhail Gorbachev.

In the 1987 general election, Thatcher won an unprecedented third term in office. But controversial policies, including the poll tax and her opposition to any closer integration with Europe, produced divisions within the Conservative Party which led to a leadership challenge. In November 1990, she agreed to resign and was succeeded by John Major as party leader and Prime Minister.

In 1992, Thatcher left the House of Commons for the House of Lords as Baroness Thatcher of Kesteven.

Text D   Boris Johnson's Speech on Brexit

Read the following passage and finish the following exercises.

1) Boris Johnson believes all Britons feel hopeful for the prospect after Brexit. The statement above is _____ (true / false).
2) The Brexit may deliver changes by controlling _____ or creating _____ or _____ the fishing industry or _____ free trade deals.
3) Johnson believes leaving the European Union is the _____ and _____ and _____ thing to do.
4) According to Johnson, by leaving the European Union the UK can regain the power of _____ and take back the tools of _____.

Tonight, we are leaving the European Union.

For many people this is an astonishing moment of hope, a moment they thought would never come. And there are many, of course, who feel a sense of anxiety and loss.

And then, of course, there is a third group—perhaps the biggest—who had started to worry that the whole political wrangle would never come to an end.

I understand all those feelings, and our job as the government—my job—is to bring this country together now and take us forward. And the most important thing to say tonight is that this is not an end, but a beginning. This is the moment when the dawn breaks and the curtain goes up on a new act in our great national drama. And yes, it is partly about using these new powers—this recaptured sovereignty—to deliver the changes people voted for, whether that is by controlling immigration or creating freeports or liberating our fishing industry or doing free trade deals, or simply making our laws and rules for the benefit of the people of this country. And of course, I think that is the right and healthy and democratic thing to do. Because for all its strengths and for all its admirable qualities, the EU has evolved over 50 years in a direction that no longer suits this country. And that is a judgment that you, the people, have now confirmed at the polls, not once but twice.

And yet this moment is far bigger than that. It is not just about some legal extrication. It is potentially a moment of real national renewal and change. This is the dawn of a new era in which we no longer accept that your life chances—your family's life chances—should depend on which part of the country you grow up in. This is the moment when we really begin to unite and level up. Defeating crime, transforming our NHS, and with better education, with superb technology and with the biggest revival of our infrastructure since the Victorians, we will spread hope and opportunity to every part of the UK. And if we can get this right, I believe that with every month that goes by, we will grow in confidence, not just at home but abroad.

And in our diplomacy, in our fight against climate change, in our campaigns for human rights or female education or free trade, we will rediscover muscles that we have not used for decades, the power of independent thought and action, not because we want to detract from anything done by our EU friends—of course not. We want this to be the beginning of a new era of friendly cooperation between the EU and an energetic Britain. A Britain that is simultaneously a great European power and truly global in our range and ambitions. And when I look at this country's incredible assets, our scientists, our engineers, our world-leading universities, our armed forces, when I look at the potential of this country waiting to be unleashed, I know that we can turn this opportunity into a stunning success. And whatever the bumps in the road ahead, I know that we will succeed.

We have obeyed the people. We have taken back the tools of self-government. Now is the time to use those tools to unleash the full potential of this brilliant country and to make better the lives of everyone in every corner of our United Kingdom.

Know More

1. What did the Whigs and Tories stand for in the early 19th century?

The Whigs was a derogatory name for cattle drivers, while Tories (an Irish word) meaning thugs. The Whigs were opposed to absolute monarchy and supported the right of religious freedom for Nonconformists. The Whigs later formed a coalition with dissident Tories in the mid 19th century and became the Liberal Party.

The Tories supported hereditary monarchy and were reluctant to remove kings. They were the forerunners of the Conservative Party, which still bears the nickname today.

2. 10 Downing Street is the residence and office of the Prime Minister of the United Kingdom of Great Britain and Northern Ireland, situated on Downing Street in the City of Westminster, central London. It is actually the official residence of the First Lord of the Treasury, but in modern times this post has always been held simultaneously with the office of Prime Minister.

Notes

1. **Harold Macmillan** (1894—1986): He was a British Conservative politician and Prime Minister of the United Kingdom from January 10 1957 to October 18 1963. Nicknamed "Supermac", in his premiership he advocated a mixed economy, championed the use of public investment to create expansion, and presided over an age of affluence marked by high growth and low unemployment. He restored the special relationship with the United States, decolonised much of  Africa, ended National Service, strengthened the nuclear deterrent, and pioneered the Nuclear Test Ban with the Soviet Union, but his unwillingness to disclose United States nuclear secrets to France led to a French veto of the United Kingdom's entry into the European Economic Community. When asked what represented the greatest challenge for a statesman, Macmillan replied: "Events, my dear boy, events."

2. **Edward Heath** (1916—2005): He is often known as Ted Heath, was Prime Minister of the United Kingdom from 1970 to 1974 and leader of the Conservative Party from 1965 to 1975. Heath's accession represented a change in the leadership of the Conservative party, from aristocratic figures such as Harold Macmillan and Lord Home to the self-consciously meritocratic Heath, and later, Margaret Thatcher. He is remembered as being the Prime Minister who took Britain into the European Economic Community (EEC) in 1973.

3. **John Major** (1943—): He is a British politician who was Prime Minister of the United Kingdom and Leader of the Conservative Party during 1990 to 1997. During his time as Prime Minister, the world went through a period of transition after the end of the Cold War.

For Fun

Movies to see

Yes Minister—BBC TV series. James Hacker, the British Minister for Administrative Affairs, tries to do something and cut government waste, but is continually held back by the smart and wily Permanent Secretary, Sir Humphrey Appleby.

The Iron Lady—An elderly Margaret Thatcher talks to the imagined presence of her recently deceased husband as she struggles to come to terms with his death while scenes from her past life, from girlhood to British Prime Minister, intervene.

Unit 4

Food and Drinks in the U.K.

> Thank God for tea! What would the world do without tea!
> How did it exist? I am glad I was not born before tea.
>
> —William Gladstone

Unit Goals

- To get a general knowledge of the food and drinks in Britain
- To get to know some traditional British ways of eating and drinking
- To develop critical thinking and intercultural communication skills
- To learn useful words and expressions concerning eating and drinking and improve English language skills

Before You Read

As drinking tea is so popular in Britain, it is not surprising that it has given rise to a number of idioms. See if you can match the meanings with the idioms.

1. not for all the tea in China
2. not my cup of tea
3. a storm in a teacup

a. making a fuss about something unimportant
b. not what I like or not what I am suited for
c. under no circumstances

Use suitable idioms to complete the following sentences.

1. I don't know why they are arguing about such a trivial matter—it's all _____.
2. Beijing is such a wonderful city. I should never live anywhere else, _____!

3. I can't stand listening to jazz. It's just _____.

Start to Read

Text A   Food and Drinks in the U.K.

1 "A nice cup of tea, the stronger the better" is **supposed** to be the British cure for all problems. Although many different drinks can be found in Britain, a cup of hot tea in the cool English climate has been a favorite of the British ever since Assam tea was discovered in India. In the mid-1800s, the Duchess of Bedford, who got hungry before dinner, started having a small meal with her afternoon *cuppa*. Soon **bakers** began making special pastries for teatime.

2 Workers coming home from factories made "high tea" their early supper, eating **toad-in-the-hole** (sausages cooked in a pancake-like batter), or **Welsh rarebit** (a melted cheese mixture served on toast). But for most of England today, tea is at 4 p.m. It starts with a pot of tea **served** with sugar and milk and includes thin slices of bread and butter, **muffins**, or **scones** with jam. Sometimes little sandwiches with egg, cucumber, or tomato are served, along with a **pudding**.

3 Although more and more British people are drinking coffee or taking wine, there are still many well-known drinks produced in the British Isles: **Stout** (so dark that it is almost black, a kind of beer from Ireland); brown **ale** (from the North of England); **whisky** (from the hills of Scotland); **cider** (made from apples pressed and **fermented**, and it comes from the West Country); the local rough cider ("scrumpy", straight from the barrel, and it is particularly strong).

4 The British love their puddings and pies, both sweet and **savoury**. A steak and kidney pudding, **steamed** for hours, is a delicious and **filling** meal. In the north of England, where leek growing competitions are here, it is possible to have a meal which is nothing but leeks in a suet crust.

5 Pork pies, with their firm **pastry** shells, are marvelous for a picnic. In Cornwall, potatoes and meat are packed into a pastry case, traditionally half-moon shaped to fit the miner's pocket, with a **ridge** for his grimy hands to hold. This is called a Cornish pasty.

6 **Porridge**, which is eaten with salt, not sugar in Scotland; Irish stew, with potatoes cooked in the same pot as the meat; Welsh **laver** bread made with seaweed and eaten for breakfast—the **variety** of historic dishes is enormous. But the most famous of them all must be roast beef and Yorkshire pudding. Sirloin of beef, **tender** and **rare**, light golden Yorkshire puddings, **crisp** green boiled cabbage, and potatoes roasted under the joint to absorb the dripping. This is the traditional British Sunday dinner.

7 **Haggis** is very popular in Scotland. There are several reasons for this. It is cheap; the main **ingredients**—oats and sheep—both grow well in the northern climate. It is particular to Scotland, being made from the bits of sheep that less careful people would throw away or **convert** into dog food. Most important of all, Robert  Burns wrote a poem about it. Burns was obviously in favour of haggis and since anything Burns approved of has to be good, it has become **elevated** to the status of the national dish. Myths have grown up around the haggis. They say it is actually a small animal with two short legs on one side and two long legs on the other. This is why it can run around hills. The way to catch a haggis is to hide behind a bush and jump out in front of it shouting "Boo!" This will cause it to turn round and so overbalance and roll down the hill into the arms of your friends with haggis-bags. They say this to tourists. If you come to Scotland as a tourist, tell them you've heard it.

After You Read

Knowledge Focus

1. **Put the following words into different sorts.**

stout	cabbage	scone	cucumber
cider	lettuce	muffin	ale leek

Tea Pastry: _____

Drink: _____

Vegetable: _____

Language Focus

1. Use the following words and expressions to complete the sentences.

convert	be supposed to	serve	flourish
in favour of	elevate	approve of	fill

1) Many people in the west, especially Christians, are not _____ death penalty.

2) I'm starving. Do you have something that can _____ my stomach?

3) —Where shall I sleep?

　　—Don't worry. We can _____ the sofa into a bed.

4) Are we _____ tip the cab driver?

5) Reading good books can help _____ our minds.

6) We are not allowed to _____ alcohol in this club.

7) Do you _____ sacrificing comfort to appearance?

8) The company has _____ since the new technique was introduced.

2. Fill in each blank with a suitable preposition or adverb.

1) "A nice cup of tea, the stronger the better" is supposed to be the British cure _____ all problems.

2) For most of England today, tea is at 4 p.m. It starts _____ a pot of tea served _____ sugar and milk and includes thin slices of bread and butter.

3) Cider, made _____ apples pressed and fermented, comes from the West Country.

4) A steak and kidney pudding, steamed _____ hours, is a delicious and filling meal.

5) In Cornwall potatoes and meat are packed _____ a pastry case, traditionally half-moon shaped to fit the miner's pocket.

6) Haggis is particular to Scotland, being made _____ the bits of sheep that less careful people would throw _____ or convert _____ dog food.

7) Burns was obviously _____ favour of haggis and since anything Burns approved _____ has to be good, it has become elevated to the status of the national dish.

8) The way to catch a haggis is to hide _____ a bush and jump _____ in front of it shouting "Boo!"

3. Proofreading and error correction.

　　The passage contains FIVE errors. Each indicated line contains a maximum of ONE error. In each case, only ONE word is involved.

If we survey eating out in Britain today, we see proliferation of so-called ethnic restaurants—Indian, Chinese, Thai, French, Italian and so on—many of them were originally opened to serve immigrant communities in Britain, but they have come to enjoy widespread popularity. Aside from these, probably the most remarked upon culinary import has been the very familiar American fast food outlet, it continues to be the source of anti-American sentiment for many who resent the Americanization of British eating. If we look at eating habits inside people's homes we see a similar picture of diversity, with pizzas and burgers and a whole global range of ready meals lie in fridges and freezers alongside British staples.

1) _____

2) _____

3) _____

4) _____

5) _____

Comprehensive Work

1. **Pair Work: Study the following British idioms about food and try to use them to make dialogues.**

    1) to spread the butter too thick
    2) to quarrel with one's bread and butter
    3) to be in a jam
    4) to run one's legs like jelly
    5) to have a finger in every pie
    6) the proof of the pudding is in the eating
    7) to save someone's bacon
    8) to ginger up
    9) to be in apple-pie order
    10) a mouse potato
    11) to be as like as two peas
    12) not one's cup of tea

    a. the test is whether it works or not
    b. to put life into, to stir up
    c. someone who spends a lot of time amusing him or herself by playing computer games, programming, etc
    d. to be clean, tidy, well-organized
    e. to find fault with one's livelihood
    f. to flatter, exaggerate one's praise
    g. not to one's taste
    h. to take a meddlesome interest in many affairs

i. to be indistinguishable from one another

j. to be in great difficulties

k. to exhaust oneself running around

l. to get someone out of a difficulty

2. Essay Writing

Write a passage of about 300 words, answering the following question.

❖ What other aspects do you enjoy about food in the U. K. beside what has been covered in the text?

Read More

Text B   British Meals

Read the following passage and finish the following exercises.

1) Which of the following is usually NOT included in a continental breakfast?

A. Croissant.   B. Baked beans.   C. Cheese.   D. Coffee.

2) If a meal is eaten in the late morning instead of both breakfast and lunch, it is called _____.

3) A ploughman's lunch is a traditional lunch for _____: a bread roll, Cheddar cheese, Branston pickle and salad, perhaps with a pork pie.

4) Many people have a tea-break at about _____ in the morning (elevenses). Tea-time is a small meal eaten in the late _____. High tea is a light meal eaten in the early _____ served with a pot of tea; this is popular in north England and Scotland.

5) _____ is the most common name for the meal eaten in the evening. _____ is another common name for _____, but sometimes it is also used to refer to lunch, especially when this is the main meal of the day.

6) British people enjoy eating _____ between meals. These include sweets and crisps.

The first meal of the day in the morning is breakfast (usually eaten between about 7:30 and 9:00). Many British people eat toast with butter or margarine and jam, or marmalade. Melon, grapefruit or fruit cocktail are popular. Others eat a bowl of cereal; for example, cornflakes or muesli with milk, or porridge (a mixture of oats, hot milk and sugar). A traditional English breakfast (also known as a cooked breakfast or a fry-up) is a cooked meal which may contain food such as sausages, bacon, kippers, black  pudding, scrambled or fried or poached egg, mushrooms, fried tomatoes, baked beans, hash browns and toast. People sometimes eat a boiled egg, dipping strips of toast into the egg yolk. A continental breakfast is a small meal and is not cooked; for example, a bread roll or croissant with cheese or ham and a cup of coffee. The most common drinks at this time of day are orange juice or a cup of breakfast tea.

Many people have a tea-break at about 11:00 in the morning (elevenses). If a meal is eaten in the late morning instead of both breakfast and lunch, it is called brunch.

Lunch is the meal eaten in the middle of the day (usually between about 12:30 and 2:00). Many people eat a sandwich. Some people have a simple meal such as cheese and biscuits or soup and bread. A ploughman's lunch is a traditional lunch for farmers: a bread roll, Cheddar cheese, Branston pickle and salad, perhaps with a pork pie. It is also traditional for people to go to a pub with some friends for a pub lunch and a drink.

A Sunday roast is a traditional meal eaten by a family at Sunday lunchtime, for example, roast beef with roast potatoes, parsnips, peas, Brussels sprouts, green beans, Yorkshire pudding, bread sauce and gravy. Mint sauce or redcurrant jelly is often eaten with lamb, apple sauce with pork, and horseradish sauce (a type of mustard) with beef, cranberry sauce with turkey. Stuffing may be eaten with chicken or turkey.

Tea-time is a small meal eaten in the late afternoon (usually between about 3:30 and 5:00). People may drink tea, and often eat biscuits, cakes or savoury foods such as sandwiches, crumpets or tea-cakes. Occasionally people may have a full afternoon tea or a cream tea: this includes a scone with jam and cream as well as a selection of sandwiches and cakes.

High tea is a light meal eaten in the early evening (for example, 6 o'clock) served with a pot of tea; this is popular in north England and Scotland. Supper is the most common name for the meal eaten in the evening (usually between 7:00 and 8:30). Dinner is another common name for supper, but sometimes it is also used to refer to lunch, especially when this is the main meal of the day. A dinner party is a formal evening meal to which guests have been invited. A common type of cooked meal in Britain is meat and two veg. This is a meat dish served together on the same plate with two types of vegetable, one of which is often a type of potato. It is common to eat a dessert after the main dish.

It is increasingly popular for British people get a takeaway or go to a restaurant instead of cooking at home, and often this is used as a chance to try different types of food. Most towns have an Indian restaurant, serving foods such as curry and chicken tikka masala. Chinese restaurants are also very common; popular dishes include sweet and sour pork and aromatic duck. Many people like Italian pizza and pasta dishes. Fast food restaurants often serve beefburgers or fried chicken. Fish and chip shops are still popular, especially in towns by the coast. There is an old tradition of eating fish on Friday.

British people enjoy eating snacks between meals. These include sweets and crisps.

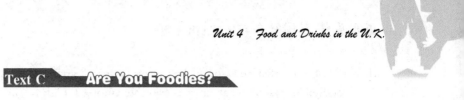

Text C   Are You Foodies?

By Kate Fox

Read the following passage and then finish the exercises.

1) How do you understand the English relationship with food as "loveless marriage"?

2) How are "foodies" treated in most other cultures?

3) What might "foodieness" suggest in English culture?

4) Foodieness is roughly <u>on a par with</u> an enthusiastic interest in fashion or soft furnishings. The underlined phrase means _____.

5) Agree or Disagree? Share ideas with your partner on the following points:

   a. Foodieness is somewhat more acceptable among females. _____

   b. It is a shame to be deeply fascinated by or passionate about food. _____

   c. We should "eat to live" rather than "live to eat." _____

"Loveless marriage" is not an entirely unfair description of the English relationship with food, although marriage is perhaps too strong a word: our relationship with food and cooking is more like a sort of uneasy, uncommitted cohabitation. It is ambivalent, often discordant, and highly fickle. There are moments of affection, and even of passion, but on the whole it is fair to say that we do not have the deep-seated, enduring, inborn love of food that is to be found among our European neighbours, and indeed in most other cultures. Food is just not given the same high priority in English life as it is elsewhere. Even the Americans, whose "generic" (as opposed to ethnic) food is arguably no better than ours, still seem to care about it more, demanding hundreds of different flavours and combinations in each category of junk food, for example, whereas we will put up with just two or three.

In most other cultures, people who care about food, and enjoy cooking and talking about it, are not singled out, either sneeringly or admiringly, as "foodies." Keen interest in food is the norm, not the exception: what the English call a "foodie" would just be a normal person, exhibiting a standard, healthy, appropriate degree of focus on food. What we see as foodie obsession is in other cultures the default mode, not something unusual or even noticeable.

Among the English, such an intense interest in food is regarded by the majority as at best rather odd, and at worst somehow morally suspect—not quite proper, not quite right. In a man, foodie tendencies may be seen as unmanly, effeminate, possibly even casting doubt upon his sexual orientation. In this context, foodieness is roughly on a par with, say, an enthusiastic interest in fashion or soft furnishings. English male "celebrity" chefs who appear on television tend to go out of their way to demonstrate their masculinity and heterosexuality: they use bloke-ish language and adopt a tough, macho demeanour; parade their passion for football; mention their wives, girlfriends or children ("the wife" and "the kids" in bloke-speak); and dress as scruffily as possible. Jamie Oliver, the young TV chef who has done so much to make cooking a more attractive career choice for English boys, is a prime example of this "please note how heterosexual I am" style, with his cool scooter, loud music, sexy model wife, Cockney brashness and laddish "Chuck in a bi' o'

this an' a bi' o' that and you'll be awright, mate" approach to cookery.

Foodieness is somewhat more acceptable among females, but it is still noticeable, still remarked upon—and in some circles regarded as pretentious. No-one wishes to be seen as too deeply fascinated by or passionate about food. Most of us are proud to claim that we "eat to live, rather than living to eat"—unlike some of our neighbours, the French in particular, whose excellent cooking we enjoy and admire, but whose shameless devotion to food we rather despise, not realizing that the two might perhaps be connected.

Text D   Pub Etiquette

Read the following passage and finish the following exercises.

1) Normally people go to a pub with other people, and it is common for one person to _____ to buy drinks for the others, especially at the beginning. This is known as buying a _____ of drinks.

2) It is common to offer a tip to the person at the bar (a barman or barmaid). The statement above is _____ (true/false).

3) In the U.K., smoking is not allowed in enclosed public places. The statement above is _____ (true/false).

4) If you bump into someone and they spill their drink, you should _____.

5) The pub is not allowed to serve drinks after closing time. You must stop drinking _____ (20/30) minutes after closing time; if you have not left _____ (on/by) this time, the pub landlord may ask you to leave.

Pubs are where many British people meet to talk and have a drink. You have to be 18 years old to order a drink in a pub. Some pubs will allow people over 14 years old to go inside if they are with someone who is over 18, but they are not allowed to go to the bar or to have an alcoholic drink (16 and 17 year olds can sometimes order an alcoholic drink with a table-meal). Family pubs welcome people with children and have facilities for them. Avoid using rough language in a family pub. Normally people go to a pub with other people, and it is common for one  person to offer to buy drinks for the others, especially at the beginning. This is known as buying a round of drinks. You should always offer to return the favour, either by paying for a round of drinks yourself, or by offering to buy a drink for the person who paid for your drink. Sometimes people each pay money (for example: 10 pounds) to one member of the group at the beginning of the evening and use this pot or kitty to pay for drinks when wanted, until the money is finished.

It is not common to offer a tip to the person at the bar. If you want, you can tell a member of the bar staff to "have a drink on me," meaning that you will pay for the drink that he/she chooses (if you are offered a drink on the house, the pub pays for it).

Bans on smoking in enclosed public places (including pubs, bars and restaurants) were introduced throughout the U. K. in 2006 and 2007. You must go outside the building (for example to the pub garden, if it has one) if you want to smoke.

If you bump into someone and they spill their drink, you should offer to buy them another one.

Opening times depend on the conditions of the pub's licence. Standard opening times are between 11 a. m. and 11 p. m. (10:30 p. m. on Sundays or on public holidays; Scottish pubs generally do not open on Sunday afternoons). Since November 24 2005, pubs can apply to extend these hours (opening earlier or closing later), so check the times when you arrive. Many places with extended hours open an hour earlier or close an hour later (e.g. at midnight). Only a few places are open all night.

About 10 minutes before closing time (at about 10:50 p. m.), the landlord will ring a bell and will tell people to order their last drinks (usually saying "Last drinks at the bar" or "Time, gentlemen, please"). The pub is not allowed to serve drinks after closing time. You must stop drinking 20 minutes after closing time. If you have not left by this time, the pub landlord may ask you to leave.

Below are some examples of some typical expressions, which you might hear or want to say when you go to a pub.

Asking someone to go out for a drink with you:
"Would you like to come out for a beer?" or "Shall we go for a drink after class/after work?"
Asking if you can buy a drink for someone:
"Do you want a drink?" or "What would you like to drink?"
"What are you having?" or "What can I get you?"
"Would you like another drink?"
Replying to someone's offer to buy you a drink:
"Can I have the same again, please?" (if the person who is offering knows what you have been drinking)
"A pint of lager, please" or "Could you get me a vodka and orange?" (specifying a particular drink)
"I'm fine, thank you." (which means you don't want another drink)
"I'm fine at the moment, thank you." (which means that you do not want another drink until later)
What the barman or barmaid might say to you:
"What can I get you?" or "Ice and lemon?" or "Anything else?"
What you may ask the barman or barmaid:
"Hello. Two pints of lager, a Tetley's Bitter and a packet of cheese and onion crisps, please."

Know More

Proper Eating Behavior Tips in Britain
- When being entertained at someone's home, it is nice to take a gift for the host and hostess. A bottle of wine, a bunch of flowers or chocolates are all acceptable.
- On arrival in a restaurant or at a formal function, give your coat to the waiter, never hang it on the back of your chair.
- Elbows should not be on the table until after all courses have been cleared away. Never lean on your elbows! Keep your posture erect.
- Your serviette should always be placed on your lap, and don't tuck it into the collar of your shirt.
- Break bread and rolls with your fingers not with your knife.
- You may use a piece of bread on a fork to soak up sauce or gravy. Never hold the bread in your fingers to do this.

Notes

1. William Gladstone (1809—1898): He was a British Liberal party statesman and four times Prime Minister (1868—1874, 1880—1885, 1886 and 1892—1894). He was a champion of the Home Rule Bill which would have established self-government in Ireland. The British statesman was famously at odds with Queen Victoria for much of his career. She once complained, "He always addresses me as if I were a public meeting." Gladstone was known affectionately by his supporters as the "Grand Old Man" or "The People's William." He is still regarded as one of the greatest British Prime Ministers, with Winston Churchill and others citing Gladstone as their inspiration.

2. Robert Burns (1759—1796): He is also known as Rabbie Burns, Scotland's favourite son, the Ploughman Poet, the Bard of Ayrshire and in Scotland as simply The Bard. He was a poet and a lyricist. He is widely regarded as the national poet of Scotland, and is celebrated worldwide. He is the best known of the poets who have written in the Scots language, although much of his writing is also in English and a "light" Scots dialect, accessible to an audience beyond Scotland.

For Fun

Movies to see

 Ratatouille—Remy is a young rat in the French countryside who arrives in Paris, only to find out that his cooking idol is dead. When he makes an unusual alliance with a restaurant's new garbage boy, the culinary and personal adventures begin despite Remy's family's skepticism and the rat-hating world of humans.

Toast—The ultimate nostalgia trip through everything edible in 1960's Britain. No matter how bad things get, it seems impossible not to love someone who made you toast.

Unit 5
The British Ways and Manners

> Good manners and soft words have brought many a difficult thing to pass.
>
> —Sir John Vanbrugh
>
> You can get through life with bad manners, but it's easier with good manners.
>
> —Lillian Gish

Unit Goals

● To learn the typical British ways in different aspects of life
● To get acquainted with the British manners of doing things
● To develop critical thinking and intercultural communication skills
● To learn useful words and expressions concerning the British ways and manners and improve English language skills

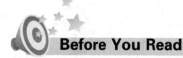

Before You Read

Typically British: Match the following descriptions with the items.

a) On every British breakfast table, a kind of jam made with oranges or other citrus fruits.	1) Pubs

| b) Time to eat cream and jam and cake at four p.m. | 2) Double-decker buses |

c) Much more than a place for a drink. They have a relaxing atmosphere in which you can chat with your friends, have a snack, and perhaps play a game of darts.

3) Marmalade

d) In London their drivers are famous for their knowledge of the streets of the city.

4) Tea Time

e) Usually red. You get a good view when you ride on the top.

5) Cabs

Start to Read

Text A　　Politeness in Britain

1 On the whole, British habits of politeness are very informal. All politeness is based on the elementary rule of showing **consideration** for others, and **acknowledging** the consideration they show to you.

2 "Excuse me" is used as an advance apology for troubling somebody, as when passing in front of him or interrupting his conversation, or when putting a question to a stranger. "Sorry" expresses regret for an **accidental disturbance** or **breach** of manners. It also takes the place of "no" when you cannot agree to a request or an implied **request** like "May I borrow your pen?" or "Do you know the time?" or "Have you any size seven shoes?" "Pardon?" is the polite way of asking somebody to repeat what he has said. In Britain, except at school, "please" is no longer used in asking **permission** to speak, and the phrase "No, please" so common abroad would sound most unusual in Britain itself. "Yes, please" is the commonest use of the word, and is the opposite of "No, thank you" when replying to an offer. A **bare** yes or no is considered very rude in this case. Similarly, a polite request does not begin with "I want" or "I think," but with a phrase like "Will (or Would, Can, Could) you please...?" or "Would you mind...?" When the request is **granted**, and at any time when you are receiving something, you are always expected to say "Thank you" however obviously you are **entitled** to it.

3 British people do not readily ask each other to do anything that would involve real **inconvenience**: they prefer to wait for such service to be offered rather than ask for it. If they do ask, then the request is accompanied by an implied apology like, "I don't really like asking you, but..." or, "I know the trouble I'm causing you, but would you mind...?" and so on. Similarly, it is often polite to refuse an offer of service by means of such a reply as "Oh! Please don't bother," followed by an explanation of why you can do without it. In fact, without being **conscious** of it, British people sometimes make offers purely out of politeness, not really expecting them to be accepted, and offers of this kind are refused with the same politeness.

4 If you are invited into a person's home, there are other questions to consider. For instance, what time should you arrive? If it is a social occasion, not a business one, it is not polite to arrive early. Your **hostess** will be preparing for you, and will be most **embarrassed** if you arrive before she is quite ready. Ten minutes late is excellent. Half an hour late is **excessive** and requires

"You were lucky to catch us in-we didn't know you were coming"

apologies. Then too, the British are rather **particular** about table manners. The main thing is: to sit up straight, copy everyone else, **gaily** asking what to do if you are not sure, and keep the conversation going. What time should you leave? There are no rules, but it is most impolite to stay too late, as it implies a lack of consideration for your hosts. If it is simply an invitation to an evening meal and conversation, you will probably take your leave between ten and eleven o'clock. If you have been asked to stay for several days, you will **conform** as far as possible to the **routine** of the house, and your hostess will be very pleased if you give her a **bunch** of flowers, specially bought, before you leave.

5 Politeness towards women is less **observed** today than it used to be. It is still considered polite to give up one's seat to a woman who is standing, to open doors for her, help her **alight** from the bus, carry things for her, protect her from the traffic, and so on, and the **maxim** "Ladies first" is well known. But now that women are the **equals** of men in having the vote, taking paid employment and receiving higher education, they receive much less consideration than formerly, for the whole basis of politeness towards women is the feeling that they need protection.

6 The same **principle** applies to old people. If they are respected in Britain, it is because they are felt to be in need of protection and support. Old age and

seniority alone do not command authority among the British, and in fact modern life has been developing so fast that old people often appear tiresome and out of date. Thus, "We need some young blood" is often heard in organizations where the energy and modern methods of younger men are felt to be more likely to succeed than the long but partly **irrelevant** experience of older ones. The wisest of the older generation realize this. They either make an effort to remain young in heart and keep pace with the times, or else they let younger men take their place.

7 It follows that **mature** Europeans have no desire to grow old or to look older than they are. Women especially, for reasons of sexual attraction, **long** to "stay young" and there is no greater **compliment** to a mature woman than to be told "How young you look!" On the other hand, if a woman's hairstyle, make-up and clothes **reveal** an obvious effort to look **artificially** young, she is said to "look common," and is regarded with **disapproval**.

After You Read

Knowledge Focus

1. Match the following occasions with proper expressions.

To ask somebody to repeat what he has said	Excuse me
To gently refuse an offer	Sorry
To make an advance apology for troubling somebody	Would you please...
To express regret for an accidental disturbance	Pardon
To make a polite request	No, thank you.

2. Mark each statement with T if it is true or F if it is false.

1) Britons prefer to wait for the service to be offered rather than ask for it. _____

2) When British people make offers, they do expect them to be accepted. _____

3) For an informal visit of one's home in the U. K., it is not polite to arrive early. _____

4) In the U. K., politeness towards women is still observed today as it used to be. _____

5) Old age and seniority alone do not command authority among the British. _____

Language Focus

1. **Use the following words and expressions to complete the sentences.**

take the place of	be entitled to	take one's leave
conform	breach	routine
out of date	keep pace with	be particular about
compliment		

1) Tom only had a mouthful of food and then _____ in a hurry.
2) Her boss paid her a _____ because of her diligence.
3) Home remedies should not _____ visiting your doctor if you are really sick.
4) You've committed a serious _____ of the regulations.
5) The manager is very _____ his clothes.
6) All are _____ an equal start.
7) It's important for a firm to _____ changes in the market.
8) She found it difficult to establish a new _____ after retirement.
9) Enterprises that fail to _____ to standards will face severe punishment.
10) Cassette tape recorders are _____ now.

2. **Fill in the blanks with the proper form of the words in the brackets.**

1) He has never shown much _____ (consider) for his wife's needs.
2) Our meeting was quite _____ (accident).
3) It's illegal to read people's private letters without _____ (permit).
4) Please accept our apologies for any _____ (convenient) we have caused.
5) He is my _____ (seniority) by two years.
6) That is a separate issue and _____ (relevant) to our discussion.
7) I noticed a slight frown of _____ (approval) on his face.
8) What did he say in _____ (explain) of his stupid behavior?

3. **Fill in each blank with a suitable preposition or adverb.**

1) _____ the whole, British habits of politeness are very informal.
2) "Excuse me" is used when putting a question _____ a stranger.
3) In fact, without being conscious _____ it, British people sometimes make offers purely _____ _____ politeness, not really expecting them to be accepted.
4) Your hostess will be preparing _____ you, and will be most embarrassed if you arrive before she is quite ready.
5) The British are rather particular _____ table manners.
6) If it is simply an invitation to an evening meal and conversation, you will probably take your leave _____ ten and eleven o'clock.
7) If you have been asked to stay _____ several days, you will conform as far as possible _____ the routine of the house.
8) The same principle applies _____ old people. If they are respected in Britain, it is because they are felt to be _____ need of protection and support.

4. Proofreading and error correction.

The passage contains FIVE errors. Each indicated line contains a maximum of ONE error. In each case, only ONE word is involved.

<table>
<tr><td>

  The English have clearly chosen a high appropriate aspect of our own familiar natural world as a social facilitator: the capricious and erratic nature of our weather ensures that there is always something new to comment on, surprised by, speculate about, moan about, or, perhaps most importantly, agree about. It brings us to another important rule of English weather-speak: always agree. This rule is noted by the Hungarian humorist George Mikes, who wrote that in England "You must never contradict somebody when discussing the weather." We have already established that weather-speak greetings or openers such as "Cold, isn't it?" must be reciprocated, but etiquette also requires that the response express agreement, like in "Yes, isn't it?" or "Mmm, very cold."

</td><td>

1) _____

2) _____

3) _____

4) _____

5) _____

</td></tr>
</table>

Comprehensive Work

1. Clear up the mix-ups.

In cross-cultural encounters between Chinese and English native speakers, the use of names and titles can be confusing. Can you identify the mistaken use of names and titles in the following cases?

Case 1

A British tourist is traveling by train in China. Sitting opposite him is a Chinese passenger. They introduce themselves to each other...

Chinese passenger: Hello, my name is Yang Fan. Glad to meet you.

British tourist: Hello, Mr. Fan. I'm Eric Jackson. Glad to meet you, too.

Chinese passenger: Where do you come from, Mr. Eric?

British tourist: I'm from England. Please just call me Eric.

Chinese passenger: And you may just call me Yang Fan.

Case 2

A British tourist is visiting a Chinese family. The Chinese hostess introduces herself and her husband to the guest...

Chinese hostess: Welcome to my home. My name is Bai Ling, and this is my husband.

British tourist: Thank you, Mrs. Bai. It's my pleasure to meet you. I'm Lucy Taylor.

Chinese hostess: Have a seat, Madam Lucy.

2. Essay Writing

Write a passage of about 300 words, presenting your understanding of the following questions.

❖ Do you recognise the British people as people with good manners?

❖ What do you expect from a person with good manners?

Read More

Text B   The Rules of Introduction

By Kate Fox

Read the following passage and write T if the statement is true and F if it is false.

1) For the English greetings and introductions are usually an awkward business. _____

2) The "How do you do?" greeting is still very commonly used by the English people nowadays. _____

3) Among established friends, there is less awkwardness in greetings. _____

4) Air-kiss is usually used by both men and women. _____

5) Handshakes are usually the norm in business introductions. _____

6) The English do not want to know your name, or tell you theirs, until a much greater degree of intimacy has been established. _____

Grooming-talk starts with greeting-talk. Weather-speak is needed in this context partly because greetings and introductions are such an awkward business for the English. The problem has become particularly acute since the decline of "How do you do?" as the standard, all-purpose greeting. The "How do you do?" greeting—where the correct response is not to answer the question, but to repeat it back, "How do you do?", like an echo or a well-trained parrot—is still in use in upper-class and upper-middle circles, but the rest are left floundering, never knowing quite what to say. Instead of sneering at the old-fashioned stuffiness of the "How do you do?" ritual, we would do better to mount a campaign for its revival: it would solve so many problems.

Awkwardness Rules

As it is, our introductions and greetings tend to be uncomfortable, clumsy and inelegant. Among established friends, there is less awkwardness, although we are often still not quite sure what to do with our hands, or whether to hug or kiss. The French custom of a kiss on each cheek has become popular among the chattering classes and some other middle- and upper-middle-class groups, but is regarded as silly and pretentious by many other sections of society, particularly when it takes the form of the "air-kiss." Women who use this variant (and it is only women; men do not air-kiss, unless they are very camp gays, and even then it is done "ironically") are disparagingly referred to as "Mwah-Mwahs." Even in the social circles where cheek-kissing is acceptable, one can still never be entirely sure whether one kiss or two is required, resulting in much awkward hesitation and bumping as the parties try to second-guess each other.

Handshakes are now the norm in business introductions—or rather, they are the norm when people in business are introduced to each other for the first time. Ironically, the first introduction, where a degree of formality is expected, is the easiest. (Note, though, that the English handshake is always somewhat awkward, very brief, performed "at arm's length," and without any of the spare-hand involvement—clasping, forearm patting, etc. —found in less inhibited cultures.)

At subsequent meetings, particularly as business contacts get to know each other better, a handshake greeting often starts to seem too formal, but cheek-kisses would be too informal (or too pretentious, depending on the social circle), and in any case not allowed between males, so we revert to the usual embarrassed confusion, with no-one being quite sure what to do. Hands are half-extended and then withdrawn or turned into a sort of vague wave; there may be awkward, hesitant moves towards a cheek-kiss or some other form of physical contact such as an arm-touch—as no contact at all feels a bit unfriendly—but these are also often aborted half-way. This is excruciatingly English: over-formality is embarrassing, but so is an inappropriate degree of informality (that problem with extremes again).

The No-name Rule

In purely social situations, the difficulties are even more acute. There is no universal prescription of handshakes on initial introduction—indeed, they may be regarded as too "businesslike"—and the normal business practice of giving one's name at this point is also regarded as inappropriate. You do not go up to someone at a party (or in any other social setting where conversation with strangers is permitted, such as a pub bar counter) and say "Hello, I'm John Smith," or even "Hello, I'm John." In fact, the only correct way to introduce yourself in such settings is not to introduce yourself at all, but to find some other way of initiating a conversation—such as a remark about the weather.

The "brash American" approach: "Hi, I'm Bill from Iowa," particularly if accompanied by an outstretched hand and beaming smile, makes the English wince and cringe. The American tourists and visitors I spoke to during my research had been both baffled and hurt by this reaction. "I just don't get it," said one woman. "You say your name and they sort of wrinkle their noses, like you've told them something a bit too personal and embarrassing." "That's right," her husband added. "And then they give you this tight little smile and say 'Hello'—kind of pointedly not giving their name, to let you know you've made this big social booboo. What the hell is so private about a person's name, for God's sake?"

I ended up explaining, as kindly as I could, that the English do not want to know your name, or tell you theirs, until a much greater degree of intimacy has been established—like maybe when you marry their daughter. Rather than giving your name, I suggested, you should strike up a conversation by making a vaguely interrogative comment about the weather (or the party or pub or wherever you happen to be). This must not be done too loudly, and the tone should be light and informal, not earnest or intense. The object is to "drift" casually into conversation, as though by accident. Even if the other person seems happy enough to chat, it is still customary to curb any urges to introduce yourself.

Eventually, there may be an opportunity to exchange names, providing this can be achieved in a casual, unforced manner, although it is always best to wait for the other person to take the initiative. Should you reach the end of a long, friendly evening without having introduced yourself, you may say, on parting, "Goodbye, nice to meet you, oh—I didn't catch your name?" as though you have only just noticed the omission. Your new acquaintance should then divulge his or her name, and you may now, at last, introduce yourself—but in an offhand way, as though it is not a matter of any importance: "I'm Bill, by the way."

One perceptive Dutch tourist, after listening attentively to my explanation of this procedure, commented: "Oh, I see. It is like *Alice Through the Looking Glass*: you do everything the wrong way round." I had not thought of recommending Alice as a guide to English etiquette, but on reflection it seems like quite a good idea.

The "Pleased to Meet You" Problem

In a small social gathering such as a dinner party, the host may solve the name problem by introducing guests to each other by name, but these are still awkward moments, as the decline of "How do you do?" means that no-one is quite sure what to say to each other when introduced in this manner. "How are you?" despite having much the same meaning, and being equally recognised as a non-question (the correct response is "Very well, thank you" or "Fine, thanks" whatever your state of health or mind), will not do in initial introductions, as custom dictates that it may only be used as a greeting between people who already know each other. Even though it does not require an honest answer, "How are you?" is far too personal and intimate a question for first-time introductions.

The most common solution, nowadays, is "Pleased to meet you" (or "Nice to meet you" or something similar). But in some social circles—mainly upper-middle class and above, although some at the higher end of middle-middle are affected—the problem with this common response is that it is just that: "common," meaning a lower-class thing to say. The people who hold this view may not put it quite like this—they are more likely to say that "Pleased to meet you" is "incorrect," and you will indeed still find etiquette books that confirm this. The explanation offered by some etiquette books is that one should not say "Pleased to meet you" as it is an obvious lie: one cannot possibly be sure at that point whether one is pleased to meet the person or not. Given the usual irrationalities, dishonesties and hypocrisies of English etiquette, this seems unnecessarily and quite uncharacteristically scrupulous.

Whatever its origins or dubious logic, the prejudice against "Pleased to meet you" is still quite widespread, often among people who do not know why it is that they feel uneasy about using the phrase. They just have a vague sense that there is something not quite right about it. But even among those with no class prejudice about "Pleased to meet you," who believe it is the correct and polite thing to say, this greeting is rarely delivered with ringing confidence: it is usually mumbled rather awkwardly, and as quickly as possible—"Plstmtye." This awkwardness may, perversely, occur precisely because people believe they are saying the "correct" thing. Formality is embarrassing. But then, informality is embarrassing. Everything is embarrassing.

Text C   What's Typically British

Read the following passage and decide whether the following statements are true or false. Write T if the statement is true and F if it is false.

1) Gardening still remains the most popular hobby in Britain. _____
2) Fish and chip shops used to be the only take-away food shops in Britain. _____
3) Most British families still keep the habit of sitting down together for breakfast. _____
4) Before the early 19th century, traffic drove on the left in most European countries. _____
5) The summer season in Britain is not as pleasant as it used to be in the past. _____

Breakfast

British people used to sit down to a traditional cooked breakfast which consisted of cereals or porridge, followed by fried eggs, fried bread, sausages, bacon, fried tomatoes, fried mushrooms and even kippers. Then you had toast and marmalade and lots of tea. Nowadays, however, most people just grab a cup of coffee and a piece of toast standing up in the kitchen, before rushing off to school or work. In fact, only one in eight families sits down together for breakfast.

Gardening

The British have always loved gardens. Walk down any street on a summer evening and everybody's out watering or weeding. In fact, until television arrived, gardening used to be the most popular hobby in Britain. Many people would say that still is, but apparently, two out of three Britons consider gardening to be "outside housework."

Driving on the left

Until the early 19th century, traffic used to drive on the left in most European countries. But nowadays they have all changed over to the right, all except Britain. Fortunately, visitors to Britain soon get used to looking right instead of left when you cross the road.

Fish and chips

Fish and chip shops used to be the only take-away food shops in Britain. The food was wrapped in newspaper and eaten with your fingers. Today there is a lot more choice. People have got used to eating Indian, Chinese, Italian and American "fast" food.

Summer

The season which sometimes comes to Britain but usually does not. But at least the rain gets warmer. August is, in fact, the third wettest month of the year. British people are used to it but they still complain. Older people, in particular, love to grumble about it: "Summer didn't use to be as bad as this when I was a child!"

Tea

Tea used to be much more popular than coffee. Although much more coffee is drunk now, six out of ten hot drinks consumed in Britain are tea, usually made with tea bags and milk. Many foreigners still believe that the whole country comes to a standstill at 5 o'clock when the British have their tea. Perhaps, this used to be true, but not any longer.

Text D   Social Customs in Britain

Read the following passage and finish the following exercises.

1) In Britain, one is supposed to arrive a few minutes early for the following occasions EXCEPT _____.
   A. weddings   B. concerts   C. someone's house for dinner

2) In Britain, it is wise to telephone before visiting someone at home. The statement above is _____ (true/false).

3) If you receive a written invitation to an event that says "RSVP," "RSVP" means _____.

4) If you have been invited for a meal. _____, _____, or a small gift are all appropriate. A _____ note or telephone call after the visit is also considered polite.

5) When inviting guests for dinner in Britain, the host or hostess may serve the food in several ways such as _____ style, _____ style and _____ style.

Time

British people place considerable value on punctuality. If you agree to meet friends at three o'clock, you can bet that they'll be there just after three. Since Britons are so time conscious, the pace of life may seem very rushed. In Britain, people make great effort to arrive on time. It is often considered impolite to arrive even a few minutes late. If you are unable to keep an appointment, it is expected that you call the person you are meeting. Some general tips follow.

You should arrive:

* At the exact time specified—for dinner, lunch, or appointments with professors, doctors, and other professionals.
* Any time during the hours specified for teas, receptions, and cocktail parties.
* A few minutes early: for public meetings, plays, concerts, movies, sporting events, classes, church services, and weddings.
* If you are invited to someone's house for dinner at half past seven, they will expect you to be there on the dot. An invitation might state "7:30 for 8," in which case you should arrive no later than 7:50. However, if an invitation says "sharp," you must arrive in time.

Invitations

"Drop in anytime" and "come see me soon" are idioms often used in social settings but seldom meant to be taken literally. It is wise to telephone before visiting someone at home. If you receive a written invitation to an event that says "RSVP," you should respond to let the person who sent the invitation know whether or not you plan to attend.

Never accept an invitation unless you really plan to go. You may refuse by saying, "Thank you for inviting me, but I will not be able to come." If, after accepting, you are unable to attend, be sure to tell those expecting you as far in advance as possible that you will not be there.

Although it is not necessarily expected that you give a gift to your host, it is considered polite to do so, especially if you have been invited for a meal. Flowers, chocolate, or a small gift are all appropriate. A thank-you note or telephone call after the visit is also considered polite and is an appropriate means to express your appreciation for the invitation.

Dress

Everyday dress is appropriate for most visits to people's homes. You may want to dress more formally when attending a holiday dinner or cultural event, such as a concert or theatre performance.

Introduction and Greeting

It is proper to shake hands with everyone to whom you are introduced, both men and women. An appropriate response to an introduction is "Pleased to meet you." If you want to introduce yourself to someone, extend your hand for a handshake and say "Hello, I am..." Hugging is only for friends.

Dining

When you accept a dinner invitation, tell your host if you have any dietary restrictions. He or she will want to plan a meal that you can enjoy. The evening meal is the main meal of the day in most parts of Britain.

Food may be served in one of several ways: "family style," by passing the serving plates from one to another around the dining table; "buffet style," with guests serving themselves at the buffet; and "serving style," with the host filling each plate and passing it to each person. Guests usually wait until everyone at their table has been served before they begin to eat. Food is eaten with a knife and fork and dessert with a spoon and fork.

Proper Behavior Tips in Britain

● Decision-making is slower in England than in the United States; therefore, it is unwise to rush the English into making a decision.

● Privacy is very important to the English. Therefore, asking personal questions or intensely staring at another person should be avoided.

● Eye contact is seldom kept during British conversations.

● Personal space is important in England, and one should maintain a wide physical space when conversing. Furthermore, it is considered inappropriate to touch others in public.

● A business lunch will often be conducted in a pub and will consist of a light meal and perhaps a pint of ale.

● When socializing after work hours, do not bring up the subject of work.

● When dining out, it is not considered polite to toast those who are older than yourself.

● One gesture to avoid is the V for Victory sign, done with the palm facing yourself. This is a very offensive gesture.

Sir John Vanbrugh (1664? —1726): He was an English architect and dramatist, perhaps best known as the designer of Blenheim Palace and Castle Howard. He wrote two argumentative and outspoken Restoration comedies, *The Relapse* (1696) and *The Provoked Wife* (1697), which have become enduring stage favourites but originally occasioned much controversy.

For Fun

Movies to see

My Fair Lady—A misogynistic and snobbish phonetics professor agrees to a wager that he can take a flower girl and make her presentable in high society.

The Duchess—A chronicle of the life of the 18th century aristocrat Georgiana, Duchess of Devonshire, who was reviled for her extravagant political and personal life.

Unit 6

Education System in the U.K.

> Education is simply the soul of a society as it passes from one generation to another.
>
> —G. K. Chesterton

Unit Goals

● To get a general knowledge of British education system
● To get acquainted with British school life
● To identify the differences between British education system and American education system
● To develop critical thinking and intercultural communication skills
● To learn useful words and expressions concerning British education system and improve English language skills

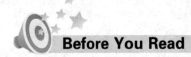

Before You Read

Work with a partner to answer the questions. Make sure you understand the meaning of the words in italics.

1) Exams at school are used as part of the *assessment* of individual performance. Do you think it is a sensible way?

2) Do you think the *vocational* training necessary for job hunters? What is your ideal *vocation*?

3) Can you name some of the most *prestigious* schools and universities in Britain? What are they?

4) Do you approve of the idea that students must wear *uniforms* at school?

5) What is $50 *equivalent* to in Chinese RMB?

6) Do you think there should be an *alternative* for College Entrance Examination?

Start to Read

| Text A | Going to School: British Style |

1 British law requires that all children attend school between the ages of 5 and 16. More than 90 percent go to what people in the United States call public schools—meaning that the school is completely or **partially funded** by the government. Less than eight percent of all British students study at **privately** funded schools. Wealthy families often send their children to **boarding** schools called (oddly enough) "public schools."

2 The British school system is considered one of the best in the world. Many other countries **model** their schools after British schools, and with good reason. More than 99 percent of all British citizens know how to read and write. All British public schools follow England's National **Curriculum** set by

the government's Department of Education and Science. Every student studies English, science, mathematics, computer science, history, geography, art, music, physical education, and a foreign language (usually French).

3 Most British students wear **uniforms**. Usually the younger children wear dark (or plaid) shorts or skirts, long socks, and a tee shirt or sweater with the school **crest**. On **assembly** or field trip days, a white shirt and dark tie **replace** the **casual** tee shirt.

4 At ages 7, 11, and 14, all British students must take three Standard **Assessment** Tests (SATs). The tests are often called Key Stage 1, Key Stage 2, and Key Stage 3. **Regardless** of a student's score, he or she will move on to the next level of schooling.

5 At 16, all English students take the GCSE (General Certificate of Secondary Education), taking examinations in 3 to 11 subjects: English, geography, French, math, philosophy, and so on. Those students who are not planning on a university education may take **vocational** subjects such as engineering. For them, their final exams are known as the NVQ (National Vocational **Qualification**) and are taken in addition to, or in place of, the GCSE. Usually, however, 16-year-old students take GCSE exams in English, math, and science. On **completion** of the exams, some students leave school and go straight to work, while others attend "Sixth Form Colleges" for further training. Those planning to attend university continue at the same school until they are 18.

6 Those preparing for university take advanced courses in one to five subjects. Classes are much smaller, and two years are spent in preparing for "A Levels" (Advanced Level Examinations). Courses focus on **specific** subjects a student hopes to study in college, and passes are required in at least three subjects. And for those who do not do well on exams but are good students, there is an **alternative**. A GNVQ (General National Vocation Qualification) requires the student to produce a **portfolio** of work. A passing grade is the **equivalent** of an "A Level." A popular GNVQ subject choice is business studies.

7 Prince William took three "A Level" exams when he was 18, the usual age for taking these tests. He passed all three—English, biology, and art history, then **submitted** his grades to several British Universities. He attended St. Andrews University in Scotland. William planned to take a year off first. Like William, some British teenagers take a "**gap** year," a break before college to travel, work (in order to earn money for college fees), or relax.

8 England has one of the oldest university systems in the world. During the 12th century, groups of scholars studied and lived together in small communities. These groups became the **foundation** for two of England's oldest and most **prestigious** universities, Oxford and Cambridge. Most university students live on campus in small single rooms some of which are more than 600 years old. Historical traditions are important to Oxford and Cambridge students, but both schools also have modern computers, science labs, and some of the finest libraries and museums in the world.

9 Students at Oxford and Cambridge do not usually attend daily lectures and labs. Everyone studies either independently or in small groups, guided by weekly sessions with a **tutor** (similar to a college instructor in the United States). Tutors **assign** weekly essays or short projects to track student progress. After three years, all students take exams and write research papers. A **faculty** committee decides if they have learned enough to graduate.

After You Read

Knowledge Focus

1. **Answer the following questions.**
   1) How many examination types are mentioned in the text? What are their respective significances?

2) How do students in Oxford and Cambridge study? What do you think of their method?

2. Fill in the blanks according to the information given by the text.

1) In Britain the compulsory education is between the ages of _____ and _____. The publicly financed schools are usually known as _____. Some students would attend another kind of school called _____.

2) At ages _____, _____, and _____, all British students must take three Standard Assessment Tests (SATs). The main examination that all students should take at 16 is the _____.

3) Those preparing for university should usually prepare themselves for _____ exams.

Language Focus

1. Use the following words and expressions to fill in the following blanks of the sentences.

model	submit	regardless of	with good reason
casual	track	alternative	in place of

1) I lost touch with most of my old school friends. With the help of internet, I have finally _____ down most of them.

2) Oh, my goodness! Can't you cook something else for a change? Shall we eat some meat _____ vegetables?

3) He _____ his manners on his father's.

4) I'm really worried, for I'm supposed to _____ the thesis to my tutor this weekend. However, I haven't written a single word.

5) He talked and talked, _____ the fact that I had been yawning one after another.

6) This kind of dress is only appropriate for _____ affairs.

7) I do want to engage myself in some pleasure. But in an obscure and lifeless place like this, I have no _____ but to sleep.

8) I'm not being unreasonable and I am angry with you _____.

2. Fill in each blank with a suitable preposition or adverb.

1) British law requires that all children attend school _____ the ages of 5 and 16.

2) Many other countries model their schools _____ British schools, and _____ good reason.

3) _____ assembly or field trip days, a white shirt and dark tie replace the casual tee shirt.

4) Regardless _____ a student's score, he or she will move on to the next level of schooling.

5) _____ completion of the exams, some students leave school and go straight to work.

6) Those preparing _____ university take advanced courses _____ one to five subjects.

7) Like William, some British teenagers take a year _____ before college to have a break.

8) Most university students live _____ campus in small single rooms.

3. Proofreading and error correction.

The passage contains FIVE errors. Each indicated line contains a maximum of ONE error. In each case, only ONE word is involved.

Universities in Britain were used to be free, but many students now have to pay for part of their course. Similarly, students used to receive a grant-money from the government in order to live. Nowadays, they have to borrow money from banks or the government, call a student loan, or take part-time jobs.

School and university life is not just about studying, however. Many students take part in drama productions or play music. Others, of course, take part in wide range of sports, such as football, rugby and cricket.

Many of the friends British people make at school and university remain friends for life, it seems to true to say that your schooldays really are "the best days of your life."

1) _____

2) _____

3) _____

4) _____

5) _____

Comprehensive Work

1. Group Work: Work with your team and share ideas with each other.

Look at the cases under School Rules below. What do you think would be reasonable solutions to the situations?

Case 1

School Uniform: The head teacher and governors of a school feel that it is important for students to be smart. They firmly support the idea of keeping the school uniform. A girl student Maria disagrees and she feels that young people at school should be free to dress as they wish. She arrives at school in a skirt out of her own choice. At 4 o'clock, she is given a note asking her parents to make sure that Maria comes to school in uniform the next day.

Case 2

Confiscation: It is close to the end of term and half the class have finished their GCSE assignments. One student brings a fashion magazine into the lesson and reads it in class. The teacher takes the magazine and tells the student to collect it at the end of term.

2. Essay Writing

Write a passage of about 300 words, presenting your understanding of the following questions.

❖ Do you agree with the idea that "Most students are socially retarded"?

❖ Why or why not?

Read More

Text B   Boarding School

Read the following passage and fill in the blanks.

1) Many of the schools accept a mixture of _____ (who live in the school grounds during term-time), _____ (who return home only at weekends) and _____ / _____ (who return home each evening), but some are only for day pupils.

2) A _____ school (usually called a prep school) is a school to prepare pupils to go to a public school.

3) A public school is an independent secondary school which is a _____ (not profit-making) and which belongs to one of the public school associations.

4) Among the most famous public schools are Eton, _____ and _____.

5) Entrance to Eton is _____ (involving or determined by rivalry), based on a test at the age of 11 and a Common Entrance exam at 13.

6) The main team sports which are played are _____ and _____ in the winter and spring, and either _____ or rowing in the summer.

7) Most of the state boarding schools are mixed sex, and they usually _____ students between the ages of 11 and 18.

8) The education in the state boarding schools is provided _____, but parents must pay for the cost of _____.

Private Boarding Schools

Independent schools do not receive funds from the government or local authorities. They charge school fees. The schools select pupils according to ability by using an entrance exam. Schools are often single-sex boys schools or girls schools, although many boys schools accept girls in the sixth form (between the ages of 16 and 18). Many of the schools accept a mixture of full boarders, weekly boarders and dayboys/daygirls, but some are only for day pupils.

A preparatory school (usually called a prep school) is a school to prepare pupils to go to a public school. Boys often

enter such schools aged about 8 and girls aged about 11. The entrance exams used by most public schools are known as Common Entrance exams and are taken at the age of 13. Some public schools have their own prep schools as well as the senior school, but students from other prep schools can apply to the senior school.

A public school is an independent secondary school which is a charity (not profit-making) and which belongs to one of the public school associations, the largest of which are the Headmasters' Conference (HMC) and the Girls' School Association (GSA). The expression "public school" can be confusing: in many countries other than England a "public school" is a school which is run by the government, which is not the case with these schools. In England the term private school is used to refer to any school which is run to make a profit. Among the most famous public schools are Eton, Harrow and Winchester.

Eton College

Perhaps the most famous public school in the U. K. is Eton. It is located near Windsor. It was founded in 1440 by the English king Henry the Sixth.

Entrance to Eton is competitive, based on a test at the age of 11 and a Common Entrance exam at 13. Academic standards are very high. The academic year starts at the end of September and has three terms. The year finishes with the exams in early June. Short courses are run at the college after the boys have left for their summer holidays. There are no girls at Eton (many other boys' public schools in the U. K. accept some girls in the upper school, after age 16). Boys leave the school at the age of 18—many go on to study at top universities such as Oxford and Cambridge.

The boys still wear a formal school uniform: a black tailcoat and waistcoat and pin-striped trousers (top hats have not been worn since the 1940s). Students at Eton are all boarders. Boys live in dormitories in a "house" (run by a "house master"). They have their own small rooms with a bed and desk. The main team sports which are played are rugby and football in the winter and spring, and either cricket or rowing in the summer. Other popular activities include drama and music. There are daily services in the chapels. Senior boys may take part in military training, or choose to do social service in the community.

State Boarding schools

There are several state boarding schools in the U. K. These can only be attended by U. K. nationals, nationals of another EU member country or those with a right to residence in the U. K. The education is provided free, but parents must pay for the cost of boarding. Most of these schools are mixed sex, and they usually cater for students between the ages of 11 and 18.

Text C   On Liberal Education

By John Henry Newman

Read the following passage and finish the following exercises.

1) According to Newman the goal of a good or liberal education is to cultivate all the following aspects EXCEPT _____.

   a. the habit of pushing things up to their first principle

   b. the instrument of good

   c. the understanding

   d. a talent for speculation and original inquiry

2) Statements from Newman. Put a tick (√) beside the statement from Newman.

   a. Though the useful is not always good, the good is always useful. _____

   b. Good is not only good, but reproductive of good; good is prolific. _____

   c. The culture of the intellect is a good in itself and its own end. _____

   d. Professional or Scientific knowledge is the sufficient end of a University Education. _____

   e. General culture of mind is the best aid to professional and scientific study. _____

   f. Education is useful which teaches us some temporal calling, or some mechanical art, or some physical secret. _____

3) What do you think is the goal of university education?

So far I readily grant, that the cultivation of the "understanding," of a "talent for speculation and original inquiry," and of "the habit of pushing things up to their first principles," is a principal portion of a good or liberal education. If then the Reviewers consider such cultivation the characteristic of a useful education, as they seem to do in the foregoing passage, it follows, that what they mean by "useful" is just what I mean by "good" or "liberal": and Locke's question becomes a verbal one. Whether youths are to be taught Latin or verse-making will depend on the fact, whether these studies tend to mental culture; but, however this is determined, so far is clear, that in that mental culture consists what I have called a liberal or non-professional, and what the Reviewers call a useful education.

This is the obvious answer which may be made to those who urge upon us the claims of Utility in our plans of Education; but I am not going to leave the subject here: I mean to take a wider view of it. Let us take "useful," as Locke takes it, in its proper and popular sense, and then we enter upon a large field of thought, to which I cannot do justice in one Discourse, though today's is all the space that I can give to it. I say, let us take "useful" to mean, not what is simply good, but what tends to good, or is the instrument of good; and in this sense also, Gentlemen, I will show you how a liberal education is truly and fully a useful, though it be not a professional, education. "Good" indeed means one thing, and "useful" means another; but I lay it down as a principle, which will save us a great deal of anxiety, that, though the useful is not always good, the good is always useful. Good is not only good, but reproductive of good; this is one of its attributes; nothing is excellent, beautiful, perfect, desirable for its own sake, but it overflows, and spreads the likeness of itself all around it. Good is prolific; it is not only good to the eye, but to the taste; it not only attracts us, but it communicates itself; it excites first our admiration and love, then our desire and our gratitude, and that, in proportion to its intenseness and fullness in particular instances. A great good will impart great good. If then the intellect is so excellent a portion of us, and its cultivation so excellent, it is not only beautiful, perfect, admirable, and noble in itself, but in a true and high sense it must be useful to the possessor and to all around him; not useful in any low, mechanical, mercantile sense, but as diffusing good, or as a blessing, or a gift, or power, or a treasure, first to the owner, then through him to the world. I say then, if a liberal education be good, it must necessarily be useful too.

You will see what I mean by the parallel of bodily health. Health is a good in itself, though nothing came of it, and is especially worth seeking and cherishing; yet, after all, the blessings which attend its presence are so great, while they are so close to it and so redound back upon it and encircle it, that we never think of it except as useful as well as good, and praise and prize it for what it does, as well as for what it is, though at the same time we cannot point out any definite and distinct work or production which it can be said to effect. And so as regards intellectual culture, I am far from denying utility in this large sense as the end of Education, when I lay it down, that the culture of the intellect is a good in itself and its own end; I do not exclude from the idea of intellectual culture what it cannot but be, from the very nature of things; I only deny that we must be able to point out, before we have any right to call it useful, some art, or business, or profession, or trade, or work, as resulting from it, and as its real and complete end. The parallel is exact—as the body may be sacrificed to some manual or other toil, whether moderate or oppressive, so may the intellect be devoted to some specific profession; and I do not call this the culture of the intellect. Again, as some member or organ of the body may be inordinately used and developed, so may memory, or imagination, or the reasoning faculty; and this again is not intellectual culture. On the other hand, as the body may be tended, cherished, and exercised with a simple view to its general health, so may the intellect also be generally exercised in order to its perfect state; and this is its cultivation.

Again, as health ought to precede labour of the body, and as a man in health can do what an unhealthy man cannot do, and as of this health the properties are strength, energy, agility, graceful carriage and action, manual dexterity, and endurance of fatigue, so in like manner general culture of mind is the best aid to professional and scientific study, and educated men can do what illiterate cannot; and the man who has learned to think and to reason and to compare and to discriminate and to analyze, who has refined his taste, and formed his judgment, and sharpened his mental vision, will not indeed at once be a lawyer, or a pleader, or an orator, or a statesman, or a physician, or a good landlord, or a man of business, or a soldier, or an engineer, or a chemist, or a geologist, or an antiquarian, but he will be placed in that state of intellect in which he can take up any one of the sciences or callings I have referred to, or any other for which he has a taste or special talent, with an ease, a grace, a versatility, and a success, to which another is a stranger. In this sense then, and as yet I have said but a very few words on a large subject, mental culture is emphatically useful.

If then I am arguing, and shall argue, against Professional or Scientific knowledge as the sufficient end of a University Education, let me not be supposed, Gentlemen, to be disrespectful towards particular studies, or arts, or vocations, and those who are engaged in them. In saying that Law or Medicine is not the end of a University course, I do not mean to imply that the University does not teach Law or Medicine. What indeed can it teach at all, if it does not teach something particular? It teaches all knowledge by teaching all branches of knowledge, and in no other way. I do but say that there will be this distinction as regards a Professor of Law, or of Medicine, or of Geology, or of Political Economy, in a University and out of it, that out of a University he is in danger of being absorbed and narrowed by his pursuit, and of giving Lectures which are the Lectures of nothing more than a lawyer, physician, geologist, or political economist; whereas in a University he will just know where he and his science stand, he has come to it, as it were, from a height, he has taken a survey of all knowledge, he is kept from extravagance by the very rivalry of other studies, he has gained from them a special illumination and largeness of mind and freedom and self-possession, and he treats his own in consequence with a philosophy and a resource, which belongs not to the study itself, but to his liberal education.

This then is how I should solve the fallacy, for so I must call it, by which Locke and his disciples would frighten us from cultivating the intellect, under the notion that no education is useful which does not teach us some temporal calling, or some mechanical art, or some physical secret. I say that a cultivated intellect, because it is a good in itself, brings with it a power and a grace to every work and occupation which it undertakes, and enables us to be more useful, and to a greater number. There is a duty we owe to human society as such, to the state to which we belong, to the sphere in which we move, to the individuals towards whom we are variously related, and whom we successively encounter in life; and that philosophical or liberal education, as I have called it, which is the proper function of a University, if it refuses the foremost place to professional interests, does but postpone them to the formation of the citizen, and, while it subserves the larger interests of philanthropy, prepares also for the successful prosecution of those merely personal objects, which at first sight it seems to disparage.

Notes

G. K. Chesterton (1874—1936): He was one of the most influential English writers of the 20th century. His prolific and diverse output included journalism, philosophy, poetry, biography, Christian apologetics, fantasy and detective fiction. Chesterton has been called the "prince of paradox." *Time* magazine, in a review of a biography of Chesterton, observed of his writing style: "Whenever possible Chesterton made his points with popular sayings, proverbs, allegories— first carefully turning them inside out."

Book to Read

The Idea of a University Defined and Illustrated：*In Nine Discourses Delivered to the Catholics of Dublin* by John Henry Newman-Regarded as the most important book on education ever written，it is a living classic that defines for groping，late-20th Century souls what it truly means to be educated.

Movies to see

The History Boys—An unruly class of gifted and charming teenage boys pursue sex，sport，and higher education.

Starter for Ten—Set in 1985，working-class student Brian Jackson（McAvoy）navigates his first year at Bristol University.

Are Our Kids Tough Enough？*Chinese School*—BBC Documentary. In a unique experiment，five teachers from China take over the education of 50 teenagers in a Hampshire school to see whether the high-ranking Chinese education system can work on British kids.

Unit 7

The British Welfare System

> I came to office with one deliberate intent: to change Britain from a dependent to a self-reliant society; from a give-it-to-me to a do-it-yourself nation; a get-up-and-go instead of a sit-back-and-wait Britain.
>
> —Margaret Thatcher

Unit Goals

● To understand the meaning of a "welfare state"
● To get a general picture of the welfare provision in contemporary Britain
● To get to know the main areas of the welfare system in Britain
● To develop critical thinking and intercultural communication skills
● To learn useful words and expressions on the welfare system in Britain and improve English language skills

Before You Read

A. Here are some key words in this unit. Look at their definitions. Put a tick to the words you already know.

_____ 1) *compulsory* required by regulations or laws

_____ 2) *welfare* health, happiness and well-being in general

_____ 3) *insurance* a means of safeguarding against risk or injury

_____ 4) *allowance* an amount of money given at regular intervals

_____ 5) *gap* a divergence or difference

B. Work with a partner. Complete each question with a word from the proceeding list. Then answer the questions.

1) Do you believe the _____ of the individual is bound up with that of the community? Why or why not?

2) How can we bridge the _____ between us and our parents?

3) Should military service be _____ in a country? Why or why not?

4) Should university students get their _____ from their parents? Why or why not?

5) Would you like to get yourself any kind of _____ service?

Start to Read

Text A — Welfare System in the U.K.

1 One day when Jerry was taking some foreign friends round London, one of them was **knocked** down by a bus. He was taken to hospital, where it was found that his **injuries** were serious. He was operated on and kept in hospital for more than a month. Specialists visited him and he was given expensive drug. When he finally left hospital, he received no bill at all, for Britain is a **welfare** state and foreign visitors receive the same free medical attention as Britons do themselves.

2 The British welfare state was planned during the Second World War by the **economist**, William Beveridge. The **Labour** government of 1945—1950 passed laws giving the country almost everything for which Beveridge asked. The **Conservative** governments which followed also accepted the Beveridge Plan and made no basic changes.

3 "Welfare" means health, comfort and freedom from **want**. A welfare state **attempts** to give all these to every member of the community, and it pays the cost out of taxes of various kinds. It is like an **immense insurance** company with which every single citizen is **compulsorily** insured.

4 The welfare service in Britain provides **allowances** and **pensions** so that no man needs fear that his family will starve if he loses his job, or falls sick, or has to retire. There are centers to which people can go for help and advice about their marriages, their children, their careers. Specially trained social workers help poor people who are in trouble.

5 When the MacDonald twins were babies, Peggy took them once a week to her local welfare center, where a doctor **examined** them, weighed them and advised her about their feeding. She could also get baby food at **reduced** prices.

6 Some people **criticize** the welfare state for being too **generous**. Others **claim** that it is not generous enough.

7 The British working man is getting too lazy, said Herbert Perkins. He stops work if he has got a pain in his toe! What we need is a bit more healthy **competition** and a bit more healthy fear of **unemployment**.

8 Elizabeth Townsend feels differently.

9 "It's true that some men can get more money from the welfare state than by working," she said, "but that's not because unemployment and family allowances are too generous. It's because our lowest paid workers get such **miserable** wages. Some of them earn only just enough to buy the **bare necessities**. Any way our family allowances are less than in most common market countries. But there's still much too big a **gap** between the top and the bottom income groups in this country."

10 Elizabeth also feels that more ought to be done for old people. She would like to see more **decent** homes and **hostels** for them. The care of lonely, **neglected** old people is one of the biggest problems of the British welfare state.

After You Read

Knowledge Focus

1. **Consider the following questions.**
   1) What happened next after one of Jerry's foreign friends was knocked down by a bus?
   2) What does "welfare" mean?
   3) Why do some people criticize the welfare state?
   4) What does Elizabeth Townsend think of the welfare system?

2. **Write T if the statement is true and F if it is false.**
   1) Only the people with British citizenship can receive free medical attention in Britain. _____
   2) While the Labour government follows the Beveridge Report, the Conservative government strongly opposes the Report. _____
   3) A welfare state entails taxes of various kinds. _____
   4) The welfare service in Britain only provides allowances and pensions for those jobless or retired people. _____
   5) In some cases, some men can get more money from the welfare state than by working. _____
   6) The care of lonely, neglected old people is one of the biggest problems of the British welfare state. _____

Language Focus

1. Complete the following sentences with the proper words and expressions.

knock down	attempt	compulsorily	neglect
criticize	gap	want	reduce

1) Education is _____ for all children in Britain between the ages of 5 and 16.

2) Our house is being _____ to make way for a new road.

3) The little boy was forced by _____ to steal a loaf of bread.

4) Nowadays, almost every family attaches the greatest importance to the child-raising, and the elderly people have been _____.

5) Before they fled the country, the enemy vainly _____ to destroy all the factories.

6) As a result, costs will be _____ by as much as 90%.

7) I think the government should take some measures to bridge the _____ between the top and the bottom income groups in this country.

8) They _____ their opponents under the cover of patriotism.

2. Collocation

Sort the following nouns into different groups according to the adj. + noun. collocation.

1) headache	2) restaurant	3) territory	4) mountain
5) improvement	6) facts	7) success	8) necessities
9) clothes	10) meal	11) fortune	12) pay
13) performance	14) behaviour	15) feet	16) weather

immense	miserable	bare	decent

3. Fill in each blank with a suitable preposition or adverb.

1) One day when Jerry was taking some foreign friends _____ London, one of them was knocked _____ by a bus.

2) The patient was operated _____ and kept _____ hospital for more than a month.

3) "Welfare" means health, comfort and freedom _____ want.

4) There are centers to which people can go _____ help and advice about their marriages, their children, their careers.

5) Specially trained social workers help poor people who are _____ trouble.

6) A welfare state attempts to give all this to every member of the community, and it pays the cost _____ _____ taxes of various kinds.

4. Proofreading and error correction.

The passage contains FIVE errors. Each indicated line contains a maximum of ONE error. In each case, only ONE word is involved.

The development of the welfare state in Britain owed much, in principle at least, the influence of the Beveridge Report of 1942. Beveridge had appointed by the wartime government to conduct a review of social security policy. However, when his report was appeared, at around the time of one of the early allied victories at El Alamein, it included, alongside a detailed blueprint for the reform of benefits, a vision for a much broader role for the state in meeting collective welfare need, captured in his famous reference to the need for public action to remove the "five giant evils" had haunted the country before the war: disease, idleness, ignorance, squalor and want.	1) _____ 2) _____ 3) _____ 4) _____ 5) _____

Comprehensive Work

1. Group Work: Work in groups of four and share ideas with group members.

Use the knowledge you have acquired about Britain's welfare system and make reference to the following pictures, list three points (at least) under both headings in the following table.

Potential or possible advantages of the Welfare State	Potential or possible disadvantages of the Welfare State

2. Essay Writing

Write a passage of about 300 words, presenting your understanding of the following questions.

❖ How do you define a functional welfare system?

❖ What changes might a good welfare system bring to people's life?

Read More

Text B   **The Welfare State**

Read the following passage and finish the following exercises.

1) It is now accepted in Britain that the state should ensure, as far as it can, that nobody should be without the means for the minimum necessities of life as the result of _____, _____, _____ or _____ families.

2) The operations of the welfare state are in four main parts.

    a. the system of _____

    b. the National _____ Service

    c. _____ benefits

    d. services for the benefit of _____

What is a "Welfare State"?

It can be defined as "a state with a government which assumes responsibility for the well-being of its citizens throughout life, through a range of interventions in the market economy." The welfare state would aim to offer its citizens:

    1) a life with certain specified standards of living which it considers reasonable and possible for all, and

"First, I'm going to wipe out poverty."

2) protection against the unexpected hazards of life (for example, losing a job, becoming sick, having an accident).

It is now accepted in Britain that the state should ensure, as far as it can, that nobody should be without the means for the minimum necessities of life as the result of unemployment, old age, sickness or over-large families.

The operations of the welfare state are in four main parts.

Firstly, there is the system of national insurance. Everybody who is working, either for himself or for an employer, is obliged to contribute a fixed amount each week to the national insurance fund; the fund which receives supplementary contributions from the proceeds of general taxation, is used for paying out benefits to people who are unemployed, or unable to earn because they are old or sick.

Secondly, free or nearly free medical and dental care is provided for everyone under the National Health Service, which is financed partly by weekly contributions paid by people who are working, but mainly by payments by the state out of general taxation.

Thirdly, supplementary benefits are provided for people whose incomes are too low for them to be able to live at a minimum standard; the system of non-contributory payments was extended and refined in 1973—1974.

Finally, there are many services for the benefit of children, apart from the provision of education. These benefits include family allowances, paid to parents in respect of each child after the first, but some subsidies for children's food have now been restricted to families who need them.

Text C   The National Health Service

Read the following passage and finish the following exercises. Write T if the statement is true and F if it is false.
1) Most of the costs of the NHS are paid for out of national insurance contributions. _____
2) The idea of the family doctor used to be strong in Britain. _____
3) There is no charge for prescribed medicine for individual patients in Britain. _____

Better known in Britain as the NHS, the National Health Service is one of the world's largest employers with over one million employees. Although some changes have been made in management since the 1980s, the principle of comprehensive and free medical treatment for all is still the central philosophy of the service based upon need rather than the ability to pay.

80% of the costs of the NHS are paid for out of general taxation, and the remainder out of national insurance contributions. Because of the increasing cost of provision, the most recent reforms have been aimed at reducing these costs. The policy has been
  ● to encourage people to use the private sector in health care and
  ● to "privatise" non-medical services, that is to employ privately-owned companies

in such jobs as cleaning, laundry etc. in state hospitals.

The idea of the family doctor has always been strong in Britain, and remains so. In order to obtain the benefits of the National Health Service, a person must normally be registered on a general practitioner's list, and if he needs medical attention, he first goes to his general practitioner or has the general practitioner come to see him. The family doctor gives treatment or prescribes medicine, or, if necessary, arranges for the patient to go to hospital or to be seen at home by a specialist. If the doctor prescribes medicine or pills, his written prescription must be taken to a chemist's shop, where the chemist prepares what is necessary. The health service funds pay for the cost of each "prescription" above the patient's contribution, but for small children and people with low incomes, there is no charge at all.

The working of the health service inevitably produces some adverse comment, and in particular it produces a good deal of form-filling and paper-work for all concerned in its operation. On the other side there are some who regret that the main objective of the service has been thwarted—though very slightly—by the fact that individual patients must pay a little towards the cost of medicine from the chemist, of glasses and some appliances, and of dental treatment. But on the whole, most British people would agree that the service is achieving its main objectives with outstanding success, though it may be a little damaged by excessive governmental economy.

Text D Health and Illness

Read the following passage and answer the following questions.
1) Why has health been a central concern of social policy in the UK, and across the world?
2) Why has NHS sometimes been dubbed by critics a national illness service?
3) Why is NHS described as a demand-led welfare service?
4) Why has the demand for health services increased in the UK?

Our health is one of the most precious features of our lives as human beings. This applies at an individual level: we all want to enjoy good health. However, it also underpins our collective interests as a society since healthy citizens make for a more successful and prosperous social order. And viewed negatively, this message is even more emphatic: poor health is debilitating and costly. It is not surprising therefore that health has been a central concern of social policy in the UK, and across the world, throughout the last two centuries of modern development; and it remains at the beginning of the twenty-first century one of the core priorities for future social policy development and public spending. Health policy is therefore at the centre of welfare planning; but at the heart our concern with health policy is a fundamental dilemma which has also underpinned much of the debate about how to develop and deliver health policy. This can be summed up in the question, "Should the focus of policy be health or illness?"

In part this is a definitional question. It is not necessarily clear what is meant by good health. For instance, should we all aspire to the standards of fitness of the professional sportsman or woman, or are overweight and inactive office workers in good health if they are actually suffering from any obvious debilitating condition? And what do we mean by illness? Illness can range from the common cold to terminal cancer, and one is clearly more serious than the other. Furthermore, illness might be separated from disease, with the latter implying the medical diagnosis of a known infection or disability and the former the unspecified symptoms experienced by individuals who feel ill. For practical purposes this distinction is captured to some extent in the way in which absence from work for sickness is treated, with the first few days being recorded as the self-diagnosed symptoms of the individual, but longer periods requiring medical diagnosis and certification of a specific condition by a doctor. The medical diagnosis of particular conditions is of course a very complex and highly specified science, but the more general terminology of health and illness is far from clearly agreed or consistently used.

More significant perhaps are the very different models of health services, and indeed the different philosophies and practices underlying these, that flow from a concern with illness rather than health. In the UK we have a National Health Service (NHS), of which more shortly, but it has sometimes been dubbed by critics a national illness service, because by and large the development and delivery of policy has been focused upon the diagnosis and treatment of sickness, rather than the promotion of good health. The vast bulk of health service resources are expended on treating patients who are ill, in particular in acute services or hospitals, with relatively little effort directed towards preventing healthy people from becoming ill in the first place. This is a balance which has been challenged by some of those working within, and outside, the NHS; and it has been subject to change over time, with the promotion of public health coming to occupy a more prominent place in health service planning in recent years. However, there is a more general consequence of the focus in practice upon treating illness rather than promoting health: it has meant that to a significant extent health provision has developed as a demand-led welfare service.

The demand-led focus of health care can be seen in the General Practitioner (GP) model that dominates primary health care. When we think that we may be ill we go to a doctor, who confirms that we are (or not), provides a diagnosis and (in most cases) prescribes some form of cure. In more serious cases, where the cure involves extensive medical intervention (an operation), the GP may refer us on to an acute service (usually a hospital), and in serious emergency cases we may go to hospital direct, generally to the accident and emergency department. In all cases, however, it is the circumstances of the citizen which determine the service provided and drive the need for resources to meet these.

When the NHS was first introduced in the UK it was assumed that access to health care for all would reduce the amount of sickness in society, and so demand on, and expenditure on, the service would gradually decline. Ironically, as we shall see, the reverse has been the case. Demand for health services has increased, leading to increased expenditure. In part this is because improved medical knowledge and techniques mean that we can treat more illnesses more effectively (though in some cases more expensively); but in part it is also to some extent the product of increasing expectations of good health and service provision amongst individual citizens. Whatever the balance here, there is no doubt that demand on the health service has driven up service provision. Yet demand for health services continues to outstrip the ability of NHS providers to meet all needs. So that, in practice, the provision of health service is often in practice a process of rationing, as revealed in the concerns over the lengths of waiting lists for treatment or the availability (or not) of expensive medicines.

Notes

William Beveridge (1879—1963): He was a British economist and social reformer. He is perhaps best known for his 1942 report *Social Insurance and Allied Services* (known as the *Beveridge Report*) which served as the basis for the post-World War II Labour government's Welfare State, especially the National Health Service.

For Fun

Book to read
The Diaries of Jane Somers by Doris Lessing—An unexpected friendship started after the loss of her mother and husband.

Movie to see
North and South—BBC TV series. Elizabeth Gaskell's passionate tale of love across the social divide.

Unit 8

The British Media

> The power of the press is very great, but not so great as the power to suppress.
>
> —Lord Northcliffe
>
> Television is an invention that permits you to be entertained in your living room by people you wouldn't have in your home.
>
> —David Frost

Unit Goals

- To understand some aspects of the mass media in Britain
- To learn about the range of newspapers in Britain
- To be familiar with the structure of broadcasting in Britain
- To develop critical thinking and intercultural communication skills
- To learn useful words and expressions concerning mass media in Britain and improve English language skills

Before You Read

Work in groups of four and share ideas with your partners.

The term mass media refers to any means or technology used to communicate a message to large groups of people.

1. Could you name some of the common means of communication we use in our daily lives? Which one is your favorite and why?

   _____

   _____

   _____

   _____

2. What do you think are the positive and negative effects of mass media?

_____

_____

_____

_____

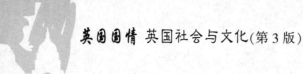

Start to Read

Text A   **The British Press**

1 If you ask an Englishman about the press in his country, he will almost certainly begin talking about the morning daily and Sunday national newspapers, all of which now have their head offices in London. Later, almost as an **afterthought**, he may go on to talk about the **provincial** morning dailies, the London and provincial evening papers, and finally the weekly local papers. The **dominating** position of the national daily morning papers is due to the smallness of the country, with every large town in England and Wales able to be reached by train in less than five hours from London. A paper printed in London around midnight can be at any breakfast table in England the next morning, except in **remote** country **districts**. All over the country,

most people read the same newspapers and the **dominant** position of the London papers may **reflect** a lack of regional **identity**.

2 The press, including weekly magazines and local newspapers, is mostly owned by one of about five large organizations. Independent small newspaper-publishers find it very difficult to **survive**, and many newspapers have stopped publication during the past twenty years—including even some national ones.

3 The number of newspapers sold, in relation to population, is higher in Britain than in any other country except Sweden. British newspaper culture is unusual in the extent to which class and educational

"Can't you take your nose out of the newspaper once in a while?"

differences are reflected in the newspapers people read. In other developed countries like Japan and the United States, newspaper reading is a mainly middle-class habit, but in Britain the "lower classes" are also **regular** readers. Among developed countries, Britain has one of the highest levels of newspaper sales per head of population, and there are over 1400 different newspapers which **cater** for a wide range of political views, interests and levels of education. Although most newspapers are **financially** independent of political parties, they often express particular political views and most people will choose to read a newspaper which **accords** with their own feelings. Thus if you were to find yourself sitting on a London tube train on a Monday morning, you would be surrounded by people reading newspapers and you could tell a great deal about your fellow passengers just by the sort of newspaper he or she was reading.

4 There are 10 different daily national papers, that is, newspapers which are **available** throughout the country and **cover issues** of national importance. About half of these are usually referred to as "the quality press." The quality press, such as *Telegraph*, *The Times*, *Guardian*, *Observer*, **carry** more serious and **in-depth** articles of particular political and social importance. They also carry reviews and **feature** articles about high culture and will generally be read by a well-educated, middle class **audience**. The other **category** of national newspapers is "the **tabloids**," smaller **format** newspapers with colour photos and **catchy headlines**. The *Mirror*, *Sun*, *Mail*, etc. belong to the type. They are often called "the **gutter** press" because they deal in **scandals** and gossip, usually about famous people, whether in politics, sports or entertainment, and carry lots of crime, sports and sensational human interest stories. The stories are short, easy to read and often rely more on opinion than fact.

5 While officially speaking the British press is "free" from government control and **censorship** and can print what it likes, there are limits to what will appear in the daily paper. In 1990, the former chairman of the KGB, the Soviet Secret Service, said, "You'll never find in a British newspaper who meets who. Not like in America—their papers are **big-mouthed**; we used to find out a lot from their press. In England, no information could be found from the papers. I always taught my people 'Do everything like the British.'"

After You Read

Knowledge Focus

1. Consider the following questions and fill in the blanks.

What are the major differences between "the quality press" and "the gutter press"?

Aspects	Types	
	Quality Press	**Gutter Press**
Contents	more _____ and _____ articles of particular _____ and _____ importance	_____ and gossip, _____ human interest stories
Features	_____ and _____ articles about _____ culture	_____ format with _____ and _____ headlines; _____ to read and often rely more on _____ than _____
Readers	a _____, _____ class audience	"_____ classes", housewives, etc.
Examples	*Telegraph*, _____, _____, *Observer etc.*	*Mirror*, *Sun*, _____ etc.

2. Write T if the statement is true and F if it is false.

1) The dominating position of the national daily morning papers is due to the smallness of the country. _____

2) The number of newspapers sold, in relation to population, is higher in Britain than in any other country. _____

3) Newspaper reading is a mainly middle-class habit in Britain and the "lower classes" seldom read newspapers. _____

4) Most newspapers are financially dependent on political parties, and they often express particular political views. _____

5) The *Mirror*, *Sun* and *Mail* belong to the type of "the quality press." _____

6) Officially speaking the British press is free from government control and censorship and can print what it likes. _____

Language Focus

1. Work with a partner to answer the questions. Make sure you understand the meaning of the boldfaced words.

1) What has made the **dominating** position of the national daily morning papers in Britain possible? _____

2) Which type of newspaper do you prefer to read, quality paper or **tabloid**? Why? _____

3) Do you wish to make friends with **big-mouthed** person? Why or why not? _____

4) What do you think might be the sensible ways to help people of **remote** country districts out of poverty? _____

2. **Use the following words and expressions to complete the sentences.**

afterthought	reflect	in relation to
independent of	deal in	carry
cater for	accord with	

1) It is very hard for a TV programme to _____ all tastes of the viewers.

2) Now that you are a college student, you should learn to be _____ your parents' help.

3) Her sad looks _____ the thought passing through her mind.

4) Our store only _____ hardware but not software.

5) All the newspapers _____ articles about the pop star's marriage.

6) What you have just said does not _____ what you told us yesterday.

7) The film was made first and the music was added as a (an) _____.

8) I have nothing to say _____ that matter.

3. **Proofreading and error correction.**

The passage contains FIVE errors. Each indicated line contains a maximum of ONE error. In each case, only ONE word is involved.

In Britain, national newspapers contribute substantially to the supposedly shared sense of it means to be "British" in a global environment. This is particular the case in Britain since unlike in other contexts such as the USA almost all the major British newspapers operate and distributed at the national level. Yet sales of British newspapers are in long-term decline. On this basis, it is commonly supposed that their influence is similar on the wane. The diminution of the power of the newspaper in Britain and worldwide seems all the more plausible we take account of the development of alternative news-delivery platforms.	1) _____ 2) _____ 3) _____ 4) _____ 5) _____

Comprehensive Work

1. **Pair Work: Work with a partner and share ideas with each other.**

1) Look at the newspaper table of contents which are reproduced from a leading British paper. Does it come from a quality or a tabloid paper? Give your reasons.

Contents	Page
Arts，Reviews	17
British News	7-10
Cartoons	23
Crosswords	23，24
European News	5
Financial News	11-13
Society	15
Law Reports	18
Letters	2
Obituary	23
Sports News	20-22
Women	16
TV，Radio，Weather	23
World News	4，6

2）Which of the following types of people would be more likely to read the *Mirror* or the *Telegraph*? Tick the appropriate box.

Job	*Mirror* readers	*Telegraph* readers
Lawyer		
Building Labourer		
Bank clerk		
Busy housewife		
Doctor		
Teacher		
Secretary		

2. Essay Writing

Write a passage of about 300 words, presenting your understanding of the following questions.

❖ Which type of newspapers do you prefer to read，"the quality press" or the tabloids?

❖ Why?

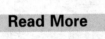

Read More

Text B　　**Contemporary British Television**

By Jane Arthurs

Read the following passage and write T if the statement is true and F if it is false.

1）British television is losing its special role as a focal point for a shared national culture. _____

2）The BBC was used simply as a propaganda tool for whoever was in political power. _____

3) Independent Television (ITV) was financed not by advertising but through a directly paid licence fee. _____

4) The second era in British television was an era of expanded choice with multi-channel systems gradually being added which offered more minority-interest programmes. _____

5) The audience has been defined by two key rhetorical figures: the "citizen" of a nation-state and the "consumer" in a global market. _____

British television was often referred to in the past as "the best in the world," but now the very idea of thinking of television as intimately bound to a sense of national pride seems almost quaint in a period where, especially for many young people, television is losing its special role as a focal point for a shared national culture. But the contribution of television to a unified British culture was of the utmost concern when the British Broadcasting Corporation (BBC) first started a television service in 1936, building on the approach it had established as the only radio broadcaster. While the BBC was always expected to be loyal to the nation-state in times of crisis or war, it was also structured to be at one remove from direct government control so that it could not be used simply as a propaganda tool for whoever was in political power. This ideal of political impartiality

"It says here that television is supposed to make you violent."

and unbiased information contributed to an ethos of television as a public service that was also free from commercial pressures, financed not by advertising but through a directly paid licence fee, offering improving education as well as entertainment for the masses. When Independent Television (ITV) was introduced in 1954, its reliance on advertising for finance was also offset by stringent public-service regulations to ensure it also fulfilled these broad aims.

This first era of television was based on a very small number of networks addressing a relatively undifferentiated, mass audience within national boundaries. The second was an era of expanded choice with multi-channel systems gradually being added which offered more minority-interest programmes. This happened gradually in the UK: the mainstream BBC and ITV terrestrial channels were supplemented by BBC 2 in 1964, Channel 4 and the Welsh language channel S4C in 1982 and Channel 5 in 1997, while the cable companies NTL and Telewest (now merged into Virgin Media) and Sky satellite television also increased capacity from the mid 1980s. There is a widespread agreement that we have now entered into a third era in television. British television is at the forefront of changes that are affecting broadcasting systems throughout the world as a result of a huge expansion in the number of channels, many of them originating from outside the UK, and its convergence with the Internet. Programmes can now be accessed via a range of interactive computer devices and watched on multipurpose screens, which vary from very small mobiles to large, flat, high-definition screens hanging on the wall, rather than the "box in the corner" that has been the norm until now. The speed of change affecting the industry has sparked a period of intense corporate and political debate over

how to adapt British television to these new economic and technological imperatives. Contested ideas about how the mixed system of public service and commercial provision should change to remain economically viable are accompanied by concerns about maintaining the quality of distinctively British programming in the face of globalising pressures.

Culturally powerful interests in the UK have over the past seventy years established and maintained television as a democratic "public sphere" as well as a conduit for popular entertainment. Debates over the relative claims of "public service" or "the market" to be able to deliver "quality" television that provides for minority as well as majority tastes and interests have recurred at regular intervals. The audience, in whose name this political wrangling is conducted, has been defined by two key rhetorical figures: the "citizen" of a nation-state and the "consumer" in a global market. These are not static categories but are open to redefinition as, for instance, new claims for citizenship emerge or new markets are exploited for profit. Neither are they entirely separate, as increasingly citizenship has become redefined in consumerist terms with the government merely providing the conditions within which private enterprise can deliver the services for which consumers pay.

The regulatory framework for this approach was established in the 2003 Communications Act, which is the most comprehensive legislation of its kind in British history. It is now being implemented by Ofcom, an organisation set up by the Government to regulate the converging communications industries, whose close relationship to government is maintained by their appointing six of its nine board members, including the chair. But whereas regulation in the past has maintained a tight control over the content of broadcasting, Ofcom's primary task has been redefined by the Government as economic regulation to promote competition. As part of this remit, they have been charged with overseeing the successful transition to a fully digital service and reviewing the provision of public-service broadcasting within the overall ecology of the British market.

Text C British Newspapers: A Ready Taxonomy of British Culture

By Michael Higgins

Read the following passage and finish the following exercises.

1) According to the passage, the "conservative values" refer to _____.

2) *The Times* is regarded as the newspaper read by _____.

3) Tabloidization refers to a form of news coverage that eschews _____ coverage in favour of an approach to journalism driven by _____.

4) The word "tabloid" originally came to denote anything that _____. In time, tabloid's establishment in the vocabulary of news production was extended to cover the characteristic: what is perceived to be _____.

5) Popular tabloids have a greater reliance on those _____.

6) _____ are of key importance in the newspaper industry to enable readers to be

accurately defined as consumers.

There is an important cultural dimension to the composition and readership of British newspapers. To take the right-wing press as our example, any temporary withdrawal of support from the Conservative Party should be seen in the context of these newspapers' continued devotion to what may be broadly defined as "conservative values," drawing on a creative fusion of individual responsibility and the free market, mixed with national belonging and hostility to foreigners. Temporary support for the Labour Party, when it is offered, is explicitly conditional upon that party's willingness to uphold the "timeless" and "common sense" standards of the political right. While it might therefore be the case that much of the press is instinctively conservative, this conservatism may be as much a commitment to a form of culture as to specific political institutions. So although there is merit in explaining the conversion of British newspapers from party allegiance to convenient politicking in terms of their response to a new, utilitarian political culture, it is also worth reflecting upon the newspapers' more established relationship with forms and distinctions in British culture as a whole.

The suggestion is that the role of newspapers in British culture is primarily a symbolic one but that they are no less important for that. Indeed, in terms of what they are seen to represent, the division and organization of British newspaper readerships offers one of the best examples we might conceive of the link between culture and politics. This correspondence between the cultural and political associations of the press is so much a part of what Stuart Hall, in another context, describes as "the common sense of the age" that it routinely passes without critical reflection. The following lines from a 1987 episode of the BBC sitcom *Yes, Prime Minster* rehearse as common knowledge the political positions of newspapers and the character of their readers:

> The *Daily Mirror* is read by people who think they run the country; *The Guardian* is read by people who think they ought to run the country; *The Times* is read by people who actually do run the country; the *Daily Mail* is read by the wives of the people who run the country; the *Financial Times* is read by people who own the country; the *Morning Star* is read by people who think the country ought to be run by another country, and the *Daily Telegraph* is read by people who think it is... *Sun* readers don't care who runs the country, as long as she's got big tits.

Although this punchline-driven comedy would be out of place in more recent BBC political satires, the list retains its ring of plausibility. Even though it has now taken to advocating political parties, *The Times* continues to be regarded as the newspaper of record, read by members of the establishment. For its part, the *Daily Telegraph* is generally thought to be purchased by those in political and cultural communion with the establishment but with the paranoia that attends the reactionary political ideologue (the above passage implies that *Daily Telegraph* readers live under the delusion that Britain is infiltrated by agents of the Soviet Union). That all such representations are to some extent gendered is apparent by the nomination of the *Daily Mail* as the paper for Conservative women. In parallel, the common political upstarts said to read the *Daily Mirror* are mocked alongside the politically apathetic and sexually puerile readers of the *Sun*. Importantly, the strict accuracy of these individual representations hardly matters. The passage succeeds in its humour because of those recognisable prejudices that attach particular newspapers with various social and political types.

However, there is another crucial element in the differentiations between the various newspapers, and that is the division between the "tabloid" and the "quality" or "broadsheet" papers. Along with the American phrase "dumbing down," tabloid journalism and "tabloidization" are terms which have been adopted internationally and across media platforms to mean a form of news coverage that eschews complex and reflective coverage in favour of an approach to journalism driven by sensationalism,  sentimentality and entertainment. In the case of the British press, "tabloid" has become interchangeable with the "popular press," a development in the composition and marketing of newspapers that Raymond Williams attributes to the emergence in the nineteenth century of the Sunday paper (the daily papers are supplemented by a set of Sunday titles, often under the same ownership) and to a concern to mix miscellany with news.

In his introduction to a light-hearted book on the press, Fritz Spiegl traces this use of "tabloid" to the registered name for a product of the pharmacists Burroughs, Wellcome & Company, who devised a form of medicine packaged in a small and easily dispatched capsule. Subsequently, the word came to be incorporated into the popular lexicon to denote anything in that comes in miniature or which is smaller than might be expected. Accordingly, Sir Thomas Sopwith's diminutive and sprightly fighter plane became known as the "Sopwith Tabloid." However, the most resilient application proved to be the new and more compact newspaper page. And as the association between "tabloid" and smaller newspapers became established, the term's employment in other situations began to recede. In time, tabloid's establishment in the vocabulary of news production saw its scope of meaning extended to cover the miniature newspapers' other characteristics: what is perceived to be a less serious approach to journalism and news. While this judgemental meaning is a contested one—at least two of the tabloid newspapers could be more accurately described as "mid-market" titles—it is to be found in the recent versions of the narratives of media malaise that have persisted since the end of the nineteenth century.

There is a compelling twist to this tale. While "tabloid" set out as a medicine designed for ease of ingestion, before going on to refer to anything that is re-presented in a smaller format, the term's development in reference to media coverage has reverted, metaphorically, to its original meaning: a form of news that will be simple to swallow. In the event, this transformation of meaning has been an appropriate one in other ways too, as the association between the "quality" newspapers and the larger, broadsheet format has itself begun to recede. In a process beginning in 2003 with *The Independent*, a number of former broadsheets began to produce their papers in the tabloid format, on the basis of its ease of handling, although all were anxious to stress that a reduction in size would not lead to a corresponding diminution of journalistic standards. Editor of *The Times*, Robert

Thompson, for example, found it necessary to reassure readers that a compacted *Times* would continue to "bring the values and the content of the broadsheet to its new shape." Trying another tactic, one paper—*The Guardian*—has even opted for a size in between (calling it "the Berliner").

Both "tabloid" and "quality" newspapers and their advertisers assume some relationship between the readership of these groups of newspapers and such attendees of social class as financial standing, where popular tabloids have a greater reliance on those in manual work with lower incomes and diminished spending power. In order that the raw figures of newspaper readership can take account of these distinctions of consumer type, an organisation known as the National Readership Survey (NRS) is commissioned to research readership demographics. The NRS is a commercial organisation run for the benefit of the publishing industry as a whole, and it provides subscribers with information on "the demographic and lifestyle characteristics" of the readers of a given publication for the purpose of selling advertising space. Through the NRS, readers are allotted to one of six "social grades" ranging from "A" (including higher managerial occupations) to "C2 and D" and "lowest grade workers" (including those on state pension and the unemployed).

In moving beyond the sheer numbers of readers that newspapers attract towards establishing what social and occupational types these bodies of readers represent, the activities of the NRS demonstrate the importance of establishing and maintaining a market position within focused income and lifestyle groups. Crucially, this is not a matter of newspapers grappling for the few most affluent readers that enjoy social prestige and limitless spending. Just as consumer products and services are designed for a range of incomes and regimes of taste so is the advertising through which these products are sold. Thus, the readership of *The Sun*—with a relatively lower average income but likely to make a markedly different set of consumer choices—is of interest to many advertisers to whom the more affluent readers of the *Daily Telegraph* or *The Times* would be deemed irrelevant. The size and social characteristics of a readership are therefore of key importance in the newspaper industry to enable readers to be accurately defined as consumers.

Text D   Drama and Documentary on British Television

Read the following passage and finish the following exercises.
1) Agree or Disagree? Share ideas with your partner on the following points.
   a. Television drama is all about ratings. _____
   b. Television drama should reflect popular culture and public taste. _____
   c. Classic programmes are more significant and should be encouraged more than the innovative, genre-breaking drama. _____
   d. Good script-writers and producers are those who have the abilities to satisfy the audiences. _____
   e. The time of the death of drama on television will come soon. _____

2) Write T if the statement is true and F if it is false.

   a. The forms of documentary practice have always been very monotonous. _____

   b. At the heart of documentary is a belief in evidence instead of authority. _____

   c. Documentary subject matter focuses simply on powerful groups and institutions. _____

   d. There is a dramatic rise in new ways of constructing documentaries. _____

   e. Innovations are highly needed for documentaries to survive new ratings wars. _____

Television Drama

Drama has been associated with BBC television since before the Second World War and with ITV since 1955. The latter, on its opening night, screened excerpts from Oscar Wilde's *The Importance of Being Earnest*. Classic drama from playwrights such as Sheridan and Ibsen featured heavily in the early days. The BBC's Sunday plays (repeated midweek) had been broadcast since the 1930s. Drama has thus always been, for the BBC, a repository for middle-class values.

In the 1990s, the subject of television drama is much debated. Critics point to a golden age of productions such as *The Forsyte Saga* and *Brideshead Revisited* and identify a decline. Recent adaptations of *Emma* and *Pride and Prejudice* have offered a rebuttal. Others disparage contemporary television drama and see Alan Bleasdale and Willy Russell as no substitute for Dennis Potter. They view even the ubiquitous sitcoms as much beneath the standards set in the 1970s and 1980s by *Fawlty Towers* and *Yes Minister*. Others welcome the way drama has begun to reach a larger audience, even though it often deals with a less sophisticated range of issues.

In what might be seen as an adverse reflection on other television drama offerings, in 1997 *East Enders* became the first soap opera to win the BAFTA award for best drama series. However, it may be that criteria for the awards have changed to reflect popular culture and public taste: television is about ratings, which may mean a move away from "quality," as it had previously been defined. Thus the shows which attracted the largest audiences may not have matched Reithian standards, but did at least reflect ordinary people's lives. The final episode of *Only Fools and Horses*, starring David Jason as Del Boy, is a case in point. It was watched by a record 24.3m people at Christmas 1996. Given that there is plenty of competition, and that audiences have a choice, ratings do reflect script-writers' and producers' abilities to satisfy.

Television is accused of relying on reruns of previous drama series. These are always "safe," and cheap, and this also suits a conservative audience who missed "classic" programmes the first time round or who like to take nostalgia trips. Despite flops like the £10m *Rhodes* and *Nostromo*, there has been much innovative, genre-breaking drama on television. Jimmy McGovern's *Hillsborough* bridged documentary, drama and reportage and led, in real life, to the reopening of the inquiry into police conduct. *This Life*, with unknown actors, bucked a trend (for example, it was suggested that the only reason for *A Touch of Frost*'s 18m viewers was the presence of star David Jason) and became an unexpected success.

All in all, the death of drama on television would seem to have been exaggerated, but most people still consider quality drama to be from the past: *The Forsyte Saga*, *Upstairs*, *Downstairs*, *Brideshead Revisited* or *The Jewel in the Crown*, for example. This was confirmed by a September 1998 *Radio Times* readers' poll, conducted to mark seventy-five years of the magazine, which found I, *Claudius* (1976) to be the "best" period drama and Ken Loach's *Cathy Come Home* (1966) the "best" single television drama.

Documentary on Television

Documentaries are broadcast regularly on British television, despite persistent fears about their diminution in a competitive climate. They are found in regular series slots on most channels, their objects of study continuing to include science, travel, wildlife, marginal groups and controversial social and political topics. Simultaneously, forms of documentary practice have become greatly diversified, so that sometimes their own workings rather than their subject matter attract public and academic discussion.

At the heart of documentary is a belief in evidence; in many programmes this is still delivered (despite various changes) by an apparently authoritative (or well-known "name") presenter, in person or through voiceover. Explorations of such topics as nuclear waste, terrorism in Northern Ireland, or prison conditions continue to provoke public discussion and, at times, government hostility. Documentary subject matter (treated incisively, or not) now includes powerful groups and institutions as well as the disadvantaged.

Some observers and film-makers see such programmes as enriched but in part displaced by a dramatic rise in new ways of constructing documentaries. These include the dramatized documentary reconstruction of political or other events ("drama-doc"), and the regular documentary treatment of the life of a hospital or other institution on a continuing basis and with key "personalities" ("docu-soap"). The availability of the lightweight camera has enabled the appearance of authored "video diaries" and of the BBC's ambitious project *Video Nation* (broadcast in two minute, half hour and longer slots) recording the views and lives of "ordinary British people", an approach which has been extended to Russian life and other subjects in parallel series.

Particularly controversial has been the evolution of the "fly on the wall" documentary, drawing on extended on-site observation sometimes with "authentically" rougher sound, jump-cutting and visible camera movements. The work of documentarists such as Molly Dineen, Roger Graef, Paul Watson and many others has embraced this kind of painstaking in-depth analysis, often through a series of institutions such as schools, the army, factories, police stations and the family. Later developments drew out the entertainment value of observing people and their foibles, so that documentaries on subjects such as shoplifting or learner car drivers began to draw very considerable audiences and even present the documentary as comedy. In the light of these innovations, much general debate continues to question the value, ethics and purpose of "serious"

documentary, together with its capacity to survive new ratings wars.

BBC

The British Broadcasting Corporation—more familiarly known as the BBC or even "the Beeb"—is Britain's main public service broadcaster. It was founded in 1927 as a public service radio station, and later moved into TV. The BBC is funded by license fees and viewers must buy a license each year for their TV set. The international arm of the BBC is the BBC World Service, which broadcasts in English and 43 other languages throughout the world.

1. **Lord Northcliffe** (1865—1922): He was a British newspaper pioneer who revolutionised magazine and newspaper publishing in Britain in the early years of the 20th century, and who wielded significant political power through the medium of his popular dailies.

2. **David Frost** (1939—2013): He is a British satirist, writer, journalist and television presenter, best known as a pioneer of political satire on television and for his serious interviews of political figures, the most notably being the interviews with Richard Nixon. As of 2009, he hosts the weekly programme *Frost over the World*, on Al Jazeera English.

3. **KGB** (Komitet Gossudarstvennoi Bezopastnosti; Committee for State Security): It was formerly the predominant security police organization of the Soviet Union. 苏联国家安全委员会(即克格勃)

Movies to see

Rag Tale—A romance that plays out in the splashy, sensational world of British tabloids.

Scoop—An American journalism student in London scoops a big story, and begins an affair with an aristocrat as the incident unfurls.

Downton Abbey—TV series from ITV. A chronicle of the lives of the Crawley family and their servants, beginning in the years leading up to World War I.

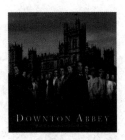

Unit 9

The Law and Justice in Britain

> If poverty is the mother of crime, stupidity is its father.
>
> —Jean de la Bruyère
>
> Let justice be done though the heavens fall.
>
> —William Watson
>
> Law is a bottomless pit.
>
> —John Arbuthnot

Unit Goals

- To understand the structure and basic principles of the British legal system
- To get to know some special features of the British judicial system
- To get acquainted with the police organization in Britain
- To develop critical thinking and intercultural communication skills
- To learn useful words and expressions concerning law and justice in Britain

Before You Read

Work with a partner and discuss the following questions.

1. Who is the lady in the picture?
2. Can you describe the lady?
3. Match exercise: What do the blindfold, scales and sword in the picture stand for?

   1) blindfold   a. fairness & equality
   2) scales   b. power & justice
   3) sword   c. impartiality

Start to Read

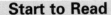

Text A   The British Legal System

1 British law has a long history, much of it being **derived** from what is called "common law." Common law has never been **precisely** defined—it is **deduced** from custom or legal **precedents** and interpreted in court by judges. This kind of law evolves long before Parliament became the main law-making body. The other kind of law, **statute** law, is law made by Parliament.

2 When a case comes before the court, each side will have a lawyer to argue their **case**. Where there have been similar cases, the court will look at these to see how they were decided. If they are practically the same, the court will follow that decision. This principle is known as "**precedence**." The idea is that there should be as much **certainty** in the law as possible. If the case is different from **previous** cases, or Parliament or the  House of Lords has changed the law, the court will have to come to a decision by interpreting any **relevant** statute law and looking at the case law to see if there are any **analogous** cases. Because of the principle of precedence, the only people who can change the law are the judges who sit in the House of Lords, the highest court, and Parliament. Parliament, however, can **overrule** the House of Lords. Certainly, judges are not supposed to make law, but to interpret it.

3 For historical reasons, the legal system in Scotland **differs** from that of the rest of the U.K. The Scottish legal system is based on Roman law, i.e. a principle applied to a case, because of the ancient **connection** with France. The system for the rest of the U.K. is based upon Norman practice, i.e. Case Law. There used to be traveling courts which **tried** cases and established precedents which were then followed by other courts. This system of precedents still continues.

4 The **administration** of justice in Britain is independent of both Parliament and the Government. Every citizen has the right to equal treatment before the law. People accused of more serious crimes are tried in open court by a judge and **jury**. Less serious cases are tried by lay **magistrates**.

5 **Lay** people play a major part in the administration of justice through the lay magistrates. People who are respected and responsible members of their local community are selected to serve as magistrates, in **county courts** within the area in which they live. They are not paid for the work and they are not professionally trained in the legal system but they do **undergo** some part-time training. There are always at least two or three magistrates in court, and up to seven may appear together. Collectively the magistrates are called the bench.

6 The jury is the other way that the public is involved in the process of justice and all **criminal trials** in the **Crown courts** and **the Old Bailey** (High Court) are held before a judge and jury. The jury represents the people and is drawn from a **cross-section** of the public. It is the jury who decide whether an accused person is **guilty** or **innocent**. The jury consists of 12 (15 in Scotland) lay people who are selected at **random** and anybody who is a **householder**, between the ages of 18—70 (65 in Scotland) can be called to serve at any time. Jury service is an **obligation** and cannot be refused except for a very strong reason.

7 In court, the jury cannot ask questions; the role of the jury is to listen **impartially** to the **evidence** from all sides. After the judge sums up all the **evidence** at the end of a trial, the jury **retire** from the court and consider their **verdict** in private. When they have reached a **unanimous** agreement of either guilty or not guilty, they return to the court and give their verdict to the judge. If the verdict is not guilty, the accused is **acquitted** and free to leave the court. If a verdict of guilty is given, the jury have no further role and the sentencing **procedure** begins. This is done by the judge alone.

8 Fines, **probation** or **imprisonment** may be **imposed** on a **convicted** person. There is a **mandatory sentence** of life imprisonment for murder throughout Britain. Life imprisonment is the **maximum** sentence of a number of other serious offences, such as **robbery**, **rape** and **manslaughter**.

9 Some people feel that there are problems **inherent** in the British legal system. Some of the traditions that have developed throughout its very long history can be seen as **out-dated** in modern society, for example the traditional dress of **wig and gown** worn by **barristers** can be seen as preserving an **unnecessary** and distancing **formality**. Others feel that the system is **elitist** since all branches of the profession are **dominated** by men from the middle and upper classes, often with a public school education, followed by university at Oxford or Cambridge. Thus other classes and **minorities** may feel that the law is **preserved** and administered by people who are not in touch

with problems found in the everyday lives of ordinary people.

After You Read

Knowledge Focus

1. Consider the following questions.

1) What are the main sources of the British law?

2) How does the British legal system work?

3) How are the lay people involved in the process of justice?

4) What are the problems inherent in the British legal system?

2. Write T if the statement is true and F if it is false.

1) Common law evolves long before Parliament became the main law-making body. _____

2) If the case is different from previous cases, the judge can work out some change on the law. _____

3) The administration of justice in Britain is dependent on both Parliament and the Government. _____

4) The administration of justice in Britain is done under a unified legal system. _____

5) The magistrates are not paid for the work and they are not professionally trained in the legal system. _____

6) For the criminal trials in the Crown courts and the Old Bailey, the judge should decide whether an accused person is guilty or innocent. _____

7) Jury service is optional in Britain, and one can decide to accept the jury duty or not. _____

8) Death penalty is the maximum sentence in Britain. _____

Language Focus

1. Use the proper words or expressions to fill in the following blanks in the sentences.

deduce	cross-section	undergo	evolve
preserve	inherent	at random	
independent	precedence	impose	

1) The people for the experiment were chosen completely _____.

2) The police _____ that the murder had been committed by a woman.

3) The researchers interviewed a _____ of the American public.

4) The magistrate _____ a fine of 500 pounds on the offender.

5) The fear of death is _____ in everyone.

6) The hospital building programme will take _____ over the road building programme.

7) I think these interesting old customs should be _____.

8) This job will make him _____ of his parents.

9) The company has _____ some major changes in the last five years.

10) According to Darwin's theory, human beings _____ from apes.

2. **Use the words in the box to fill in the blanks.**

convict	verdict	acquit	trial	jury
barrister	probation	manslaughter	evidence	
magistrate	imprisonment			

The combination of professionals and lay people in the judicial system is felt to be desirable in Britain. The judges are professionals and they must have been practicing in the legal profession as a _____ or solicitor for a certain number of years before being appointed a judge. However, _____ and the public serving on a _____ have no professional training in the law.

In criminal _____ by jury, the jury decides the issue of guilt or innocence. After considering the _____ thoroughly, the jury usually reach a unanimous decision of either guilty or not guilty. If the jury _____ is not guilty, the accused is _____ and free to leave the court.

If the accused is _____, the judge decides the level of punishment. If the offence is not very severe, the punishment like _____ may be delivered which can last between 6 months and 3 years; if the offender fails to comply with the order or commits another offence during this period, he or she can be brought before the court again. The most severe punishment in Britain is life _____ which may be given, for example, to a person guilty of murder or _____.

3. **Proofreading and error correction.**

The passage contains FIVE errors. Each indicated line contains a maximum of ONE error. In each case, only ONE word is involved.

The historic public fascination with the proceedings of the criminal justice system remains undiminished, and often fuelled by intense media activity. The courts, and specifically the image of the Central Criminal Court, The Old Bailey, remains a central dramatic forum in the narratives of everyday life. Recently, tensions between law and justice have appeared such as the image of (in)justice has cast a shadow over a number of high profile miscarriage of justice cases (such as the Birmingham Six and the Bridgewater Four). To date, the English courts have resisted the intrusion of alive television coverage that proved such controversial in the trials of Simpson and the Menendez brothers in the USA.	1) _____ 2) _____ 3) _____ 4) _____ 5) _____

Comprehensive Work

1. Group Work: Work in groups of four and share ideas with each other.

   1) What are the potential or possible advantages and disadvantages of the jury system?

Potential or Possible Advantages	Potential or Possible Disadvantages

   2) Should death penalty be justified? Why or why not?

Pros	Cons

2. Essay Writing

   Write a passage of about 300 words, presenting your understanding of the following question.

   ❖ What do you think might be the advantages of involving lay people in the judicial system?

Read More

Text B   Origins of Common Law

Read the following passage and then finish the exercises.

1) All of the following were the considerations for William the Conqueror after he conquered England EXCEPT _____.

   a. He must reward his supporters with grants of his land.

   b. He must collect rents from the landholders beneath him.

   c. He must keep the peace among both the natives and his supporters.

   d. He must fight against the church for absolute power.

2) All of the following statements are true EXCEPT _____.

   a. William conquered a relatively civilized land.

   b. William organized all the lords, church leaders, and many of the major native landlords who swore allegiance into a Great Council.

c. The Church was not involved in handling the problems of daily governance at the time.

    d. The local sheriffs were appointed in the king's name.

3) The major administrative task for William the Conqueror was to govern in his own name, namely, _____ land disputes, _____ rents, and _____ the peace.

4) It was _____ who began the actual takeover of the lower local courts.

5) This practice of the lower courts consisted of _____ the local customs of the place and time and _____ to daily events what people felt was fair. We might call this the custom of following custom. However, to judge that way would amount to judging on _____ and _____ ground.

6) Following local custom would _____ William's long-range political objectives. Hence the royal courts slowly _____ some customs and _____ others in an attempt to rule _____ in the king's name.

Put yourself in the position of William the Conqueror. You are, like many of your Norman kin, a shrewd politician. You have just managed the remarkable political feat, at least for the eleventh century, of assembling thousands of men and the necessary supporting equipment to cross the English Channel and to win title to England in battle. In these feudal days, title means ownership, and in a real sense you own England as a result of the Battle of Hastings.

However, your administrative headaches have just begun. On the one hand you must reward your supporters—and your supporters must reward their supporters—with grants of your land. On the other hand, you don't want to give up any of the land completely. You deserve to and shall collect rents—taxes are the modern equivalent—from the landholders beneath you. You must give away with one hand but keep a legal hold with the other.

Furthermore, you must keep the peace, not only among the naturally restless and resentful natives but also among your supporters. As time goes on and their personal loyalty to you dwindles, they will no doubt fight more readily over exactly who owns which lands. And, of course, you have a notion that you and your successors will clash with that other group claiming a sort of sovereignty, the Church.

You must, in short, develop machinery for collecting rents, tracking ownership, and settling disputes.

Fortunately, you have conquered a relatively civilized land. At the local level some degree of government already exists on which you can build. In what we would call counties, but which the natives call shires, a hereditary *shire reeve* (our sheriff) cooperates with a bishop representing the Church to handle many of the problems of daily governance. These shires have courts, as do the smaller villages within them. You hope that, in the next century at least, your successors will be able to take control of them.

Meanwhile you take the action of any good politician. You undertake a survey, a sort of census, of who owns what lands—the *Domesday Book*. You organize all the lords (to whom you granted large amounts of land), church leaders, and many of the major native landlords who swear allegiance to you, into a Great Council. They advise you (and you thus co-opt their support) on the important policy questions before you. You start appointing the local sheriffs yourself. You also create a permanent staff of bureaucrats—personal advisors who handle and resolve smaller problems as they arise.

You succeed in creating a new political reality, one in which it soon becomes somehow right to govern in the name of the ultimate landlord, the king.

So much for the role-playing.

William in no sense developed the contemporary common law system, but he did create the political reality in which that development had to happen: governing in the king's name—settling land disputes, collecting rents, and keeping the peace—meant rendering justice in the king's name. William's personal advisors (his staff) often traveled about the country administering *ad hoc* justice in the king's name. Additionally, many of the more serious offenses, what we would today call *crimes*, came directly to the Great Council for decision because they were offenses against the king's peace.

One hundred years later, Henry II began the actual takeover of the lower local courts. Initially, the king insisted on giving permission to the local courts before they could hear any case involving title to his land. A litigant would have to obtain from London a *writ of right* and then produce it in court before the court could hear the case. Shortly thereafter the king's council began to bypass the local courts altogether on matters of land title. Certain council members heard these cases at first, but, as they became more and more specialized and experienced, they split off from the council to form the king's Court of Common Pleas.

Similarly, the council members assigned to criminal matters developed into the Court of the King's Bench. The Court of the Exchequer, which handled rent and tax collections, evolved in similar fashion.

Some problems remained. The first concerned the rules of law these judges should use. One solution, ultimately adopted in many continental jurisdictions, was simply to use the old Roman codes. In England, however—partly because it was easy and partly because it possessed considerable local political appeal—the king's judges adopted the practice of the pre-Conquest local courts. This practice of the lower courts consisted of adopting the local customs of the place and time and applying to daily events what people felt was fair. We might call this the custom of following custom.

The custom of following custom, however, produced the second problem. In a sparsely populated area—a primitive area by today's standards of commerce and transportation—customs about crimes, land use, debts, and so forth varied considerably from shire to shire, village to village, and manor to manor. But the king's judges could hardly decide each case on the basis of whatever local custom or belief happened to capture the fancy of those living where the dispute arose. To judge that way would amount to judging on shifting and inconsistent ground. Judging would not occur in the name of the king but in the name of the location where the dispute arose. Following local custom would undercut William's long-range political objectives.

Hence the royal courts slowly adopted some customs and rejected others in an attempt to rule consistently in the king's name. Because justice in England rested on the custom of customs, the customs that the royal courts adopted and attempted to apply uniformly became the customs *common* to all the king's land. Thus the royal courts did not just follow custom; they created new common customs by following some, rejecting others, and combining yet others into new customs.

Of course, by doing this the courts no longer ruled by custom, strictly speaking. Because they sought to rule in the king's name, they sought to rule consistently. In doing so, the courts rejected some customs. Although judges no doubt felt that what they decided was right because it had its roots in some customs, it would be wiser to say they created not common custom but common law—law common throughout England.

Text C Jury System in the Dock

Read the following passage and then finish the following exercises.

1) The expression "in the dock" means _____.
2) Fill in the blanks with proper prepositions.
   a. It is a right fiercely fought _____, and fiercely defended at those times when its powers have been seen to be _____ threat.
   b. _____ being directed to by the judge and subjected _____ imprisonment, the jury refused to convict the Quaker of "leading a dissident form of worship."
3) The new proposals by the U. K. government is meant to speed up the legal process. The statement is _____. (true / false)
4) Which of the following offences will NOT be tried by the jury? _____.
   a. Murder   b. Drunkenness   c. Rape

The right to a trial by jury is a tradition that goes right to the heart of the British legal system. It is a right fiercely fought for, and fiercely defended at those times when its powers have been seen to be under threat—as those backing reforms are finding.

The tradition of being "tried by a jury of one's peers" probably has its origins in Anglo Saxon custom, which dictated that an accused man could be acquitted if enough people came forward to swear his innocence.

Trial by jury was first enshrined in law in what has been seen as the world's first proclamation of human rights—the *Magna Carta*. The document, decreed in 1215 by King John after a rebellion by his barons, stated that a "freeman shall not be... imprisoned... unless by the judgement of his peers." The right to trial by jury was finally established absolutely in the legal system following the trial of William Penn in 1670.

A jury of 12 randomly chosen citizens of London refused to convict the Quaker of "leading a dissident form of worship," despite being directed to by the judge and subjected to imprisonment and starvation in a bid to force their hand.

The latest government proposals are seen by some as a direct attack on the traditions established in the *Magna Carta* and confirmed in the Penn trial. The government wants some defendants to lose the right to choose trial by jury over magistrates' hearing. Supporters say that the reform is practical for an overburdened modern legal system. The proposed changes affect the Act of 1855 allowing some crimes to be tried by magistrates instead of a higher court if the defendant agreed. The act was designed—like the new proposals—to speed up the legal process.

The offences covered included theft, burglary, actual bodily harm and criminal damage. Minor offences, such as drunkenness, could only be tried by magistrates, and major offences, such as murder and rape, only by jury.

Text D　　The Police in Britain

Read the following passage and finish the exercises.

1) The common nickname for a British policeman is _____ (Bobby/Teddy), which is a derivation of Robert, the first name of the founder of the modern police force.

2) The Metropolitan Police Force is still in existence with its headquarters at _____.

3) Each of the local police force has its own _____. The local force is divided into the _____ branch and the _____ police.

4) Which of the following descriptions is NOT related to the police's role of *Order Maintenance*?

    a. An image of the local "bobby on the beat"

    b. Visiting local schools to give advice to children

    c. Advising local people on how to form a "Neighbourhood Watch Scheme"

    d. Enforcing the criminal law

5) Many members of the police service join trade unions. The statement is _____. (true / false)

The common nickname for a British policeman, Bobby, with its connotations of helpful and friendly assistance on the streets, is a derivation of Robert, the first name of the founder of the modern police force. The modern police force was started in 1828 in London with the establishment of the Metropolitan Police Force by Sir Robert Peel, the Home Secretary.

The Metropolitan Police Force is still in existence with its headquarters at Scotland Yard and London now also has the City of London Police Force. Since its establishment in the 19th century, the police organization has grown to 52 regional police forces, each of which has its own Chief Constable.

The local Chief Constables are in charge of their forces and are responsible for the appointment, promotion and discipline of all ranks below them, except for the assistant chief constables. They present their local police committee with an annual report and are responsible to them for the efficiency of their force.

The local force is divided into

- the uniformed branch who patrol on foot or by car and whose uniform is easily recognized; navy-blue suits and distinctive shaped helmets
- the plainclothes police, who investigate serious crime, and are known as the CID (Criminal Investigation Department)

Members of the police service are not allowed to join a trade union, nor are they allowed to go on strike. However, all ranks have staff associations to represent their interests.

What qualities are needed to be a police officer? The police may be seen as having two roles in society, each with a different emphasis and image.

- *Maintenance of order*—where the police provides a service to the community. This is known as community policing and requires the cooperation of the local community and favours an image of the local "bobby on the beat" who is known and recognised by the public in a particular area. This will involve the officer visiting local schools to give advice to children on how to avoid being a victim (for example, "not talking to strangers"), etc. The police will also advise local people on how to form a "Neighbourhood Watch Scheme" (where residents jointly agree to take it in turns to look out for suspicious behaviour and report it to the police).

a policeman

- *Law enforcement*—where the police are considered as a force with a primary function of enforcing the criminal law.

Citizens are allowed to complain about the conduct of any police officer and any wrongful treatment they may have had from the action of the police. To ensure a thorough and independent investigation of any such complaint the independent Police Complaints Authority supervises any such inquiry. Police officers breaking the law in the course of their duty can be prosecuted and even dismissed from the force. The discipline codes are designed to prevent abuse of power and to maintain public confidence in police impartiality.

Notes

1. **William Watson** (1715—1787): He was an English physician and scientist who was born and died in London. His early work was in botany, and he helped to introduce the work of Carolus Linnaeus into England. He became a Fellow of the Royal Society in 1741 and vice president in 1772.

2. John Arbuthnot (1667—1735): He was a physician, satirist and polymath in London. He is best remembered for his contributions to mathematics, his membership in the Scriblerus Club (where he inspired both Jonathan Swift's *Gulliver's Travels* book III and Alexander Pope's *Peri Bathous*, or the *Art of Sinking in Poetry*, *Memoirs of Martin Scriblerus*, and possibly *The Dunciad*), and for inventing the figure of John Bull.

For Fun

Movies to see

12 Angry Men—A dissenting juror in a murder trial slowly manages to convince the others that the case is not as obviously clear as it seemed in court. The setting of the film is in the U.S., but it helps the students in understanding the jury system in the U.K.

Runaway Jury—A juror on the inside and a woman on the outside manipulate a court trial involving a major gun manufacturer.

Legally Blonde—When a blonde sorority queen is dumped by her boyfriend, she decides to follow him to law school to get him back and, once there, learns she has more legal savvy than she ever imagined.

Unit 10

Family Life in the U.K.

> What greater thing is there for human souls than to feel that they are joined for life—to be with each other in silent unspeakable memories.
>
> —George Eliot

Unit Goals

● To get a general knowledge of family life in the U.K.
● To learn some basic values concerning the British family
● To get acquainted with some of the changes in the British family
● To develop critical thinking and intercultural communication skills
● To learn useful words and expressions concerning family life in the U. K. and improve English language skills

Before You Read

Learn some idioms about family & marriage.

1. Match each idiom with its definition.

1) to tie the knot   A. to only be able to think about one person

2) a match made in heaven   B. (a relationship that is) in difficulty

3) black sheep of the family   C. (for a characteristic) to appear in many (or all) members of a family

4) to have a crush on someone   D. get married

5) on the rocks   E. the worst member of the family

6) to run in the family .   F. a happy or harmonious marriage

2. Now complete each of the sentences by using one of the idioms above.

1) When I was at school, I _____ a film star.

2) Once she moved out, it was clear their marriage was _____.

3) Jane and Peter had exactly the same likes and interests—it was _____.

4) His father and uncle were basketball stars in college, so athletic ability _____.

5) Michael and Hannah are going to _____ next month!

6) He keeps making a nuisance of himself. What do you expect from the _____?

Start to Read

Text A   **Family Life in the U.K.**

Modern Family

1 Father leaves for work in the morning after breakfast. The two children take the bus to school, and mother stays home cooking and cleaning until father and the kids return home in the evening. This is the traditional picture of a happy family living in Britain. But is it true today?

2 The answer is no! The past 20 years have **seen enormous** changes in the lives and structure of families in Britain.

3 The biggest change has been caused by **divorce**. As many as 1 out of 3 marriages now end in divorce, leading to a situation where many children live with one parent and only see the other at weekends or holidays.

4 There has also been a huge rise in the number of women with children who work. The large rise in divorces has **meant** many women need to work to support themselves and their children. Even where there is no divorce, many families need both parents to work in order to survive. This has caused an increase in childcare **facilities**, though it is very expensive and can be difficult to find in many areas.

5 In addition, women are no longer happy to stay at home raising children, and many have **careers** earning as much or even more than men, the traditional **breadwinner**.

6 There has also been a **sharp** increase in the number of **single** mothers, particularly among teenagers. Some people have **blamed** this increase for the rise in crime. They feel that the **lack** of a **male** role model has damaged these children in society.

7 However，these changes have not had a totally **negative** effect. For women，it is now much easier to have a career and good **salary**. Although it is difficult to be a working mother，it has become **normal** and is no longer seen as a bad thing for children.

8 As for children themselves，some argue that modern children grow up more independent and mature than in the past. From an early age，they have to go to childminders or **nurseries**，and so they are used to dealing with strangers and mixing with other children.

Marriage

9 "Family" is of course an elastic word. But when British people say that their society is based on family life，they are thinking of "family" in its narrow，**peculiarly** European sense of mother，father and children living together alone in their own house as an economic and social unit. Thus，every British marriage **indicates** the beginning of a new and independent family—hence the **tremendous** importance of marriage in British life.

"You're more beautiful today than you were the day I met you. You had a really big pimple that day."

10 For both the man and the woman，marriage means leaving one's parents and starting one's own life. The man's first duty will then be to his wife，and the wife's to her husband. He will be **entirely** responsible for her **financial** support，and she for the running of the new home. Their children will be their common responsibility and theirs alone. Neither the wife's parents nor the husband's，nor their brothers or sisters，aunts or uncles，have any right to **interfere** with them—they are their own masters.

11 Readers of novels like Jane Austen's *Pride and Prejudice* will know that in former times marriage among wealthy families were arranged by the girl's parents，that is，it was the parents' duty to find a suitable husband for their daughter，**preferably** a rich one，and by skillful encouragement to lead him **eventually** to ask their **permission** to marry her. Until that time，the girl was protected and **maintained** in the parents' home，and the financial relief of getting rid of her could be seen in their giving the **newly** married pair a sum of money called a **dowry**.

12 It is very different today. Most girls today get a job when they leave school and become financially independent before their marriage. This has had two results. A girl chooses her own husband，and she gets no dowry.

After You Read

Knowledge Focus

1. Consider the following questions.

1) What was the traditional British family like?

2) What is the major cause of the changes of family?

3) What are the new changes in modern women's life?

4) What effects have the changes brought to British people's life?

5) What does marriage mean to the newly married couple?

2. Write T if the statement is true and F if it is false.

1) The past 20 years have seen little changes in the lives and structure of families in Britain. _____

2) The large rise in divorces has meant that many women need to work to support themselves and their children. _____

3) In the past, men were considered to be the breadwinner of the family. _____

4) The changes of the family have had a totally negative effect on the society. _____

5) Nowadays, children grow up more independent and mature than in the past. _____

6) In Britain, for both the man and the woman, marriage means leaving one's parents and starting one's own life. _____

7) After the children get married, both the wife's parents and the husband's have the right to interfere with their life. _____

8) In Jane Austen's time, the girl was protected and maintained in the parents' home. _____

Language Focus

1. Complete the following sentences with the proper words and expressions.

see	elastic	interfere with	eventually
maintain	tremendous	indicate	damage
mean	preferably		

1) He tries not to let his business _____ his home life.

2) The heavy rain has _____ many houses.

3) The play became a _____ hit.

4) The last 30 years have _____ considerable changes in China.

5) She _____ married the most persistent one of her admirers.

6) They want to buy a new house, near the sea _____.

7) The rules are _____. We can make some new changes.

8) He _____ his willingness with a nod of his head.

9) He's hopelessly inefficient, but I suppose he _____ well.

10) He is too poor to _____ his family.

2. **Fill in each blank with a suitable preposition or adverb.**

1) Father leaves _____ work in the morning after breakfast.

2) As many as 2 out of 3 marriages now end _____ divorce, leading _____ a situation where many children live _____ one parent and only see the other at weekends or holidays.

3) Some people have blamed this increase _____ the rise in crime.

4) As _____ children themselves, some argue that modern children grow up more independent and mature than in the past.

5) They are used to dealing _____ strangers and mixing with other children.

6) He will be entirely responsible _____ her financial support, and she _____ the running of the new home.

3. **Proofreading and error correction.**

   The passage contains FIVE errors. Each indicated line contains a maximum of ONE error. In each case, only ONE word is involved.

   Nature in every sphere of life is prodigal of reproductive capacity. Overpopulation in the animal and vegetable kingdoms is prevented by such factors like climate and shortages of food and water. Since human beings as species are, however, remarkably adept in controlling their environment and organizing supplies of necessities, the population threatens to increase to danger point if means are taken to limit excess reproductive capacities. These basic principles were stated by, for example, Thomas Malthus in his *Essay on Population* of 1798. In nineteenth-century Britain, however, material prosperity followed industrialization and colonial expansion fostered a huge expansion in population, with improving public health countered the effects of industrial pollution and epidemics in slums.

1) _____
2) _____

3) _____

4) _____

5) _____

Comprehensive Work

1. **Group Work: Work in groups of four and share ideas with group members.**
   Study the following sayings about Family. How do you understand the meanings of the sayings? What's your understanding of the family? If possible, produce a saying of your own.

   Our most basic instinct is not for survival but for family. Most of us would give our own life for the survival of a family member, yet we lead our daily life too often as if we take our family for granted.

—Paul Pearshall

If the family were a fruit, it would be an orange, a circle of sections, held together but separable—each segment distinct.

—Letty Cottin Pogrebin

Don't hold your parents up to contempt. After all, you are their son, and it is just possible that you may take after them.

—Evelyn Waugh

All happy families resemble one another, each unhappy family is unhappy in its own way.

—Leo Tolstoy

Home is the place where boys and girls first learn how to limit their wishes, abide by rules, and consider the rights and needs of others.

—Sidonie Gruenberg

Other things may change us, but we start and end with the family.

—Anthony Brandt

2. **Essay Writing**

Write a passage of about 300 words, presenting your understanding of the following questions.

❖ Common "wisdom" says that living together in a "trial marriage" is a good way to determine if couples are compatible before marriage. Do you think the idea could work out?

❖ Why or why not?

Read More

Text B   Changing Values and Norms of the U.K. Family

Read the following passage and finish the following exercises.

1) By the year 2020, it is estimated that there will be more _____ people than _____ people.

2) In the past, people _____ married and _____ married. Divorce was very difficult, expensive and took a long time.

3) Many couples, mostly in their twenties or thirties, live together without getting married. They are also called _____ couples.

4) Many women in Britain prefer to concentrate _____ their jobs and put _____ having a baby until late thirties.

The family in Britain is changing. The once typical British family headed by two parents has undergone substantial changes during the 20th century. In particular, there has been a rise in the number of single-person households, which increased from 18 to 29 percent of all households between 1971 and 2002. By the year 2020, it is estimated that there will be more single people than married people. Fifty years ago, this would have been socially unacceptable in Britain.

In the past, people got married and stayed married. Divorce was very difficult, expensive and took a long time. Today, people's views on marriage are changing. Many couples, mostly in their twenties or thirties, cohabit without getting married. Only about 60% of these couples will eventually get married.

In the past, people married before they had children, but now about 40% of children in Britain are born to cohabiting parents. In 2000, around a quarter of unmarried people

"I needed someone who would always love and adore me, always find me fascinating, someone to spoil me rotten and never leave. So I married myself!"

ohabiting in Great Britain. Cohabiting couples are also starting families without first being married. Before 1960, this was very unusual, but in 2001, around 23 percent of births in the U.K. were to cohabiting couples.

People are generally getting married at a later age now and many women do not want to have children immediately. They prefer to concentrate on their jobs and put off having a baby until late thirties.

The number of single-parent families is increasing. This is mainly due to more marriages ending in divorce, but some women are also choosing to have children as lone parents without being married.

Text C   One-Parent Family

Read the following passage and finish the following exercises.

1) Please define a "broken home": _____.
2) According to the passage, it is _____ (better/worse) for the quarreling couple to divorce each other instead of being forced to stay together just to bring up the children.
3) A one-parent family may be headed by a _____ father or mother, by a _____ or widower, by a married woman _____ from her husband, or it may be headed by a (an) _____ mother.
4) A self-help group is one in which _____.

5) Fill in each blank with a suitable preposition or adverb.

  a. The divorced parents very often marry someone else and set _____ a new family home.

  b. The children may feel they are better _____ with just one parent, or with a new step-parent.

  c. It may be difficult for the unmarried mother to bring _____ a family on her own. She may not be able to work and look _____ her child.

"You want me to clean my room. What's my budget for the project?"

    Since the Reform Act of 1969, it has been easier to get a divorce in Britain and the divorce rate has increased. There is now one divorce for every three marriages.

    The result of a divorce or separation, if there are children in the family, is a "broken home." It is usual for the children to live with their mother. Their father will probably have the legal right to visit the children and have them to stay with him for part of the school holidays. Over 1.5 million children are affected by divorce. There are, therefore, many broken homes in Britain today, but the parents very often marry someone else and set up a new family.

    So a family is no longer forced to stay together just to bring up the children. The children are often happier, too, particularly if they are used to their parents quarrelling endlessly. They may feel that they are better off with just one parent, or with a new step-parent. About 14 percent of all families with dependent children have only one parent. A one-parent family may be headed by a divorced father or mother, by a widow or widower, by a married woman separated from her husband. Or it may be headed by an unmarried mother.

    These days, an unmarried mother may choose to have a baby without marrying the father. She wants to keep the baby rather than have it adopted.

    The unmarried mother is just one of many single-parent families. But it may be difficult to bring up a family on her own. She may not be able to work and look after her child. There are some self-help groups which she can join. A self-help group is one in which all the members are in a similar situation, and they help one another.

Text D   Marriage Customs

Read the following passage and finish the following exercises.

1) Marriage in a "registry office" is _____ (more/less) formal but _____ (more/less) purely legal than a wedding in the church.

2) After the wedding, there is nearly always a "reception" consisting of a _____ (substantial/light) meal to which all the relatives and friends of the bride and bridegroom are invited. This is paid for by the _____ (groom's/bride's) parents.

3) The bond of marriage is felt to be _____ (weaker/stronger) than the bond between

the bride and her mother.

4) In Britain, the groom's family is supposed to give some money to the bride's family. The statement is _____ (true/false).

"I need you, darling. You complete me."

Most British couples, whether religious or not, have a church wedding, with the bride dressed in a long white frock. This combines the religious rite with the legal contract. Other couples are married in a "registry office," where the ceremony is less formal and more purely legal. After the wedding, there is nearly always a "reception" consisting of a light meal to which all the relatives and friends of the bride and

bridegroom are invited. This is paid for by the bride's parents. After this the newly-married couple go off on a one-or-two-week honeymoon, during which they enjoy all the pleasures and none of the responsibilities of married life.

The wedding ceremony resembles an ordinary Christian service during which the bride and bridegroom make promises to each ether, according to which, whatever unforeseen difficulties they may encounter, they will remain loyal to each other until they die. In other words, the bond of marriage is felt to be stronger than any previous family bonds, stronger even than the bond between the bride and her mother. This explains why in certain forms of service, the bride is "given away" by a close relative, usually her father. It also explains why, for the bride's mother, a daughter's wedding is sad as well as joyful. She shares her daughter's happiness, but she feels that she has lost her—the final link of filial dependence has been broken. The bridegroom's mother feels the same to a lesser extent with regard to her son, since he too has now left the family circle.

A British marriage is therefore not the lending of a girl by one family to a boy from another; it is the beginning of a third family, quite distinct from the other two, and living quite separately from them in complete financial independence. The main expense of marriage is connected with the establishment of a new home, not with the ceremony itself. No money is paid to the bride's family. The idea of a "bride price" is quite foreign to the British, which gives them the impression that the bride is a piece of merchandise to be traded, rather than a free-acting human being with the privilege of making her own decisions and living her own life.

Know More

The Wedding Vow

A wedding vow is an oath or a promise of the commitment one makes to his/her new spouse. The following is a popular sample of wedding oath.

I, ... take you, ... to be my wife (husband), to have and to hold, from this day forward, for better for worse, for richer for poorer, in sickness and in health, to love and cherish, until we are parted by death; as God is my witness. I give you my promise.

Notes

George Eliot (1819—1880): Also known as Mary Anne (Marian) Evans, she was an English novelist. She was one of the leading writers of the Victorian era. Her novels, largely set in provincial England, are well known for their realism and psychological perspicacity.

For Fun

Movies to see

Bridget Jones's Diary—A British woman is determined to improve herself while she looks for love in a year in which she keeps a personal diary.

About a Boy—Based on Nick Hornby's best-selling novel, the story of a cynical, immature young man who is taught how to act like a grown-up by a little boy.

Mamma Mia! —A young woman about to be married discovers that any one of three men could be her father. She invites all three to the wedding without telling her mother, Donna, who was once the lead singer of Donna and the Dynamos.

Unit 11

The British Sports and Games

> Serious sport has nothing to do with fair play. It is bound up with hatred, jealousy, boastfulness, disregard of all rules and sadistic pleasure in witnessing violence; in other words it is war minus the shooting.
>
> —George Orwell

Unit Goals

● To get to know some popular sports and games in Britain

● To understand British people's attachment to sports

● To appreciate the "sporting spirit" of the Britons

● To develop critical thinking and intercultural communication skills

● To learn useful words and expressions concerning sports and games in Britain and improve English language skills

Before You Read

1. **Work with a partner and share ideas with each other.**

   What reasons, apart from physical fitness, do people have for participating in different sports?

   _____

   _____

   _____

2. **Read the sentences below that contain pairs of opposites in parentheses. Choose the correct words and write them in the sentence blanks.**

   1) Football, basketball and rugby are popular _____ (individual/team) sports.

   2) Everyone calls Mary "Miss Knowledge," for she reads _____ (intensively/extensively).

3) Football is the most popular _____ (participant/spectator) sport in the world.

4) Rugby is a rough game played by teams ranging from schoolchildren to _____ (amateur/professional) players on English international teams.

5) When the idea of winning in sports is carried to excess, honourable _____ (cooperation/competition) can turn into disorder and violence.

Start to Read

Text A   The British Sports

1 Be careful when you talk to your British friends about sports. To the British, all sports, especially those involving teams, are considered serious subjects. Almost every British student plays on a school team. Many grow up and join adult **leagues**, while thousands more sit in stadiums cheering their favorite **professional** teams every weekend.

2 The game **peculiarly** associated with England is cricket. Many other games too are English in origin, but have been popularly **adopted** in other countries; cricket has been extensively adopted only in the Commonwealth, particularly in Australia, India, Pakistan and the West Indies. Nearly every village in England, except in far north, has its cricket club. A first-class match lasts for up to three days, with six hours' play on each afternoon.

3 Cricket makes no progress in **popularity**. For the majority of the British public, the eight months of the football season are more important than the four months of cricket. Professional football is always a big business. Every town has at least one professional football club. The players have not necessarily any personal connection with the town for whose team they play. The best British football players earn huge salaries, worldwide fame, and movie-star popularity. People all over the world follow the progress of their favorite British

football teams. Many travel thousands of miles to attend the Wembley Stadium **championship** games at the end of each season. In addition, British teams compete in several international matches each year.

4 The game of **rugby originated** at England's Rugby School in 1823. **Legend** says that student William Webb Ellis picked up the ball during a football game and ran with it. Today, all Rugby Union teams have 15 players positioned in two lines. Since the players do not wear pads or **protective** clothing, **bruises** and injuries are frequent. There is some professional League rugby in the north, but elsewhere rugby union is mainly played by **amateurs** and favoured by the middle class. It is also the game played at the great majority of "public school."

5 The more social adult games of golf and tennis are played by great numbers of people. Golf courses are also meeting places of the business community. It is, for example, very **desirable** for bank managers to play golf. Moreover, there are plenty of tennis clubs. Every town provides numerous **tennis courts** in public parks, and anyone can play tennis cheaply.

6 Next to Association Football, the chief **spectator** sport in English life is horse racing. Partly because of the laws which forbid such activities on Sundays, horse racing is organized rather differently in England from other countries. Their horse racing mainly takes place on working days and during working hours. The whole atmosphere of a race meeting still belongs in some ways to the eighteenth century with old **divisions** between upper and lower people. Everyday people all over the country **bet** on the day's races.

7 Although the British are so fond of watching horses racing, they are not very interested in being spectators at occasions when human beings race together. Although **athletic** sports and **gymnastics** are practiced at school, few

towns have running tracks for public use. **Remarkably** few people are interested in bicycle racing. On the other hand, **rowing**, in fours or eights, occupies a leading place in the sporting life of schools and universities which have suitable water nearby. It is watched from the river banks by vast crowds of spectators.

8 Britain was first home to many of the modern world's most popular sports. The English cannot claim, today, that they have **surpassing** skill in any form of sport when they engage in international **competition**. But they care strongly about the "sporting spirit," the **capacity** to play with respect for the rules and the opponents, to win with modesty and to lose with good temper.

After You Read

Knowledge Focus

1. **Take a guess: What is the sport?**

   1) It seems clear that the English game originated in the sheep-rearing country of the Southeast; however, it is fair to say that the real power in the game has shifted from England to ex-colonies such as Australia, New Zealand, South Africa, etc. The sport is _____.

   2) The sport is played with an egg-shaped ball. It can be a dangerous game as players wear no protective clothing. The sport is _____.

   3) The sport has always been a popular choice with the working classes because of its symbiotic relationship with gambling. The sport is _____.

   4) Today, violence is still associated with the sport. Supporters of rival teams, sometimes clash before, during and after matches and occasionally run riot through the town and beat each other up. The sport is _____.

2. **Paraphrase the following sentences.**

   1) Many other games too are English in origin, but have been popularly adopted in other countries.

   _____

   2) Cricket makes no progress in popularity.

   _____

   3) The best British football players earn huge salaries, worldwide fame, and movie-star popularity.

   _____

   4) Although the British are so fond of watching horses racing, they are not very interested in being spectators at occasions when human being race together.

   _____

   5) The English cannot claim, today, that they have surpassing skill in any form of sport when they engage in international competition.

   _____

   6) They care strongly about the "sporting spirit," the capacity to play with respect for the rules and the opponents, to win with modesty and to lose with good temper.

   _____

英国国情 英国社会与文化(第3版)

Language Focus

1. Complete the following sentences with proper words. Change the form if necessary.

peculiarly	popularity	bruise	originate
adopt	legend	desirable	division
athletic	surpassing		

1) Chinese food is becoming _____ among Americans.

2) He has become a _____ in his own lifetime for his scientific discoveries.

3) This style of cooking is _____ to the south-west of the country.

4) Our school has _____ a new teaching method.

5) The Industrial Revolution _____ from the invention of the steam engine.

6) I must admit that I cannot do it; this task _____ my ability.

7) _____ from all over the world took part in the Olympics.

8) For this job, it is _____ that you know something about medicine.

9) The river forms the _____ between the old and new parts of the city.

10) Please move the basket carefully; peaches _____ easily.

2. Match the sports with their grounds.

football   court

golf

tennis   pitch

cricket

badminton   course

rugby

3. Fill in the blanks with proper prepositions or adverbs.

1) Almost every British student plays _____ a school team.

2) The game peculiarly associated _____ England is cricket.

3) Cricket makes no progress _____ popularity.

4) Legend says that student William Webb Ellis picked _____ the ball during a football game and ran _____ it.

5) Their horse racing mainly takes place _____ working days and _____ working hours.

6) The whole atmosphere of a race meeting still belongs in some ways _____ the eighteenth century with old divisions _____ upper and lower people.

7) Everyday people all over the country bet _____ the day's races.

8) Although the British are so fond _____ watching horses racing, they are not very interested _____ being spectators at occasions when human beings race together.

4. Proofreading and error correction.

The passage contains FIVE errors. Each indicated line contains a maximum of ONE error. In each case, only ONE word is involved.

124

For the public-school-educated amateurs of the Rugby Football Union, it was the root of all evil. For the departing members of the Northern Union, as rugby league was originally called, it was made the world go round. The men who run the Northern Union had earned their money not from inheritance or landowning and from industry and business, and their commitment to amateurism was further weakened by their general values, observing Eric Dunning and Kenneth Sheard in their *Barbarians, Gentlemen and Players: A Sociological Study of the Development of Rugby Football*. That is, they were more openly achievement-oriented and acquisitive, showed a greater tendency to place money value on social relations and personal attributes.

1) _____
2) _____
3) _____
4) _____
5) _____

Comprehensive Work

1. **Group Work: Work in groups of four and share ideas with group members.**
   Read the following passage and air your opinions on "Sporting spirit." Do you share the same idea with the author, or do you think differently?

The Sporting Spirit

I am always amazed when I hear people saying that sports create goodwill between the nations, and that if only the common peoples of the world could meet one another at football or cricket, they would have no inclination to meet on the battlefield. Even if one did not know from concrete examples that international contests lead to orgies of hatred, one could deduce it from general principle.

SAY IT LOUD! WE SUCK AND WE'RE PROUD!

Nearly all sports practiced nowadays are competitive. You play to win, and the game has little meaning unless you do your utmost to win. On the village green, where you pick up sides and no feeling of patriotism is involved, it is possible to play simply for the fun and exercise; but as soon as the question of prestige arises, as soon as you feel that you and some larger units will be disgraced if you lose, the most savage combative instincts are aroused. Anyone who has played even in a school football match knows this. At the international level, sport is frankly mimic warfare. But the significant thing is not the behaviour of players but the attitude of the spectator.

2. Essay Writing

Wite a passage of about 300 words，presenting your understanding of the following question.

❖ What qualities do you think a good sportsman should possess?

Read More

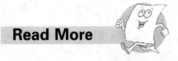

Text B　　**Cricket—A Very English Game**

Read the following passage and finish the following exercises.

1) It was the _____ of England who invented cricket，passing the time while their sheep grazed.

2) Which of the following items is NOT related to the cricket game? _____
   A. Wicket　　　B. Bats　　　C. Pitch　　　D. Stick

3) Which of the following pictograms describes the cricket game? _____

A　　　　　　　　　　　B

4) The expression "not cricket" means _____.

Although football was also invented in England and has had far wider international impact，the game of cricket is perhaps the sport which most vividly demonstrates "Englishness."

England's wealth in the Middle Ages and subsequent advantages in the development of trade and industry were initially based on wool and it was the shepherds of England who invented cricket，passing the time while their sheep grazed. They used the closely nibbled smooth green spaces as their pitch，the wooden barred gate of the sheep pen as their wicket and the crooks made from willow branches as their bats.

Cricket reminds the English of this idyllic rural scene and leisurely pace of life. The village green with the church and the pub in sight is a prevailing image of community life. A cricket match in progress on the green with the players in white shirts and white trousers，the evening sun casting the men's long shadows to the deeper shade beneath ancient trees，expresses the essentially clean，peaceful，timeless image of the countryside beloved of the English. A cricket ground in a city transplants this rural greenness into modern urban society. The sound of "leather on willow" (the bat hitting the ball) can evoke a twinge of emotion and nostalgia equivalent to hearing the cuckoo in spring.

To see real English cricket, a visitor should go to watch a village team. On Saturday and Sunday summer afternoons, on driving into any village, he is certain to hear the crack of a bat hitting a ball. Then presently he will come to a field or village green. All around it, sitting on the ground, on benches, or in their cars, are the people of the neighbourhood. They are not saying much, but their eyes are fixed on the cricket pitch.

A match between counties can take four days and a test between countries five days. As the weather in England is seldom predictable for five days in a row, this also means that the match may be abandoned or inconclusive because of "rain stop play." This gives time for interminable conversation about the weather and allows full play for demonstration of the supposed English virtues of patience and steadfastness in adverse circumstances.

Playing cricket is also meant to be synonymous with gentlemanly behaviour. It should involve fair play, team spirit and individual excellence. If any action in other spheres of life, whether in business, politics or everyday interaction does not meet these standards, particularly of honesty and fairness, it is described as "not cricket."

As with all sports, the professional game has become more sophisticated and commercialized. But cricket in its simplest form can still be seen being played in parks and back gardens throughout England, wherever there is a child big enough to hold a bat and another who can throw a ball.

Text C   The Highland Games

Read the following passage and finish the following exercises.

1) The Highland games refer to the games in _____.
   A. Northern England   B. Scotland   C. Northern Ireland

2) An enormous man wearing a kilt is trying to throw a tree trunk high into the air. The description above refers to the game _____.

3) Use proper expressions to fill in the blanks:
   If burly men throwing giant pieces of wood around are _____ (something you do not like), then perhaps the musical aspect of the Highland games would be more _____ (fitting into your interests).

4) Which of the following does NOT belong to traditional Scottish musical instruments? _____
   A. Bagpipe   B. Drum   C. Fiddle   D. Saxophone

For many foreign people the classic image of summer sport in the U. K. is that of English gentlemen dressed in white flannels playing cricket all day in the village park.

However, if you travel north of the border, to Scotland, you may find a very different kind of sporting entertainment—enormous men wearing kilts trying to throw tree trunks high into the air, or beautiful girls dancing gracefully on top of swords, all accompanied by the haunting music of the bagpipes.

This is the Highland games, a celebration of Scottish and Celtic culture which takes

place every summer in the north of Scotland. Although many Highland games take place around Scotland each summer, they all share certain common characteristics.

At the heart of any Highland games are the heavy events. These traditional sports are designed to let competitors show off their physical prowess and require great strength.

The most emblematic of the heavy events is known as "tossing the caber"—in this event a strong man throws a tree trunk (or caber), which is around 5.5 meters in length and weighs 55kg, into the air. In order to win, the caber must turn over in the air and land at a good angle to the thrower.

If burly men throwing giant pieces of wood around are not your cup of tea, then perhaps the musical aspect of the Highland games would be more to your taste.

Music and dance form an enormous part of Scottish and Celtic culture, and traditional Scottish music is immediately identifiable because of its use of traditional instruments such as the bagpipes, drums and fiddle.

Highland dancing is a competitive event in which kilted dancers try to outdo each other in terms of grace and technical achievement.

And if that is not enough, you can enjoy the sight of mock battles as historical societies recreate famous battles from Scotland's history. If you enjoyed *Brave Heart* at the cinema, you will love the Highland games in real life.

Text D   Traditional Games in Scotland

Read the following passage and finish the following exercises.

1) Of all the games played in Scotland in days gone by, three stand out as claiming Scottish origin and being particularly Scottish in character. The three games are _____, _____ and _____.

2) Tell the names of the games according to the information given.

    a. It is played with a ball made of cork and leather and a wooden club, which used to be popular amongst all ages, particularly round about the season of Christmas. _____

    b. It is played with heavy flat stones to slide along the ice, which is often referred to as "the roaring game" because of the sound resulting from the stone speeding along. _____

A love of sport has been characteristic in Highlands and Lowlands alike. It is inherent in the Scottish character. Of all the games played in Scotland in days gone by, three stand out as claiming Scottish origin and being particularly Scottish in character—golf, curling, and shinty, and of these, golf has now achieved worldwide popularity.

The best country for golf is a large expanse of uncultivated soil not too much broken up by hills; and in Scotland the links, particularly along the east coast, form ideal ground. Of all Scottish golfing centres, St. Andrews is the shrine of golfing tradition.

There is much evidence, however, that the kings and queens of Scotland themselves shared their people's enthusiasm for playing games. Queen Mary of Scots was accused by her enemies of playing golf shortly after her husband's murder. And the years before 1857 have been described as the golden age of private golf matches, for it saw the first championships inaugurated at the initiative of the Prestwick Golf Club in Scotland. It began with a letter addressed by the Prestwick Golf Club to seven leading clubs, proposing that each club should nominate four players for a golf match. The last victorious pair should be declared champions and the prize be a medal or a piece of plate. The response was enthusiastic. This began the English Amateur Golf Championship, now restricted to players born in England and the Channel Island and the sons of parents born in these places.

Curling is a game played on a sheet of ice. This sport is believed to have sprung from Holland just over four centuries ago, but Scotland has been its real home since the early part of the 17th century. In principle the game very much resembles bowls, but curling is played with heavy flat stones to slide along the ice. The oldest curling stone found in Scotland bears the data of 1511. The game is often referred to as "the roaring game" because of the sound resulting from the stone speeding along.

Like golf, curling can claim to be both royal and ancient. Tradition has it that the Stuart kings were curlers. Like golf, it too has won popularity outside Scotland, although

to a lesser extent, and there are curling clubs in England, Canada, New Zealand, Russia and Switzerland. Now curling stones are cut from hard rock, rounded and polished, and fitted with a wooden handle.

Among games less widely popular, but still played with great enthusiasm, shinty is one of the most traditional. Played with a ball made of cork and leather and a wooden club, it used to be popular amongst all ages, particularly round about the season of Christmas, but now is usually indulged in only by the more youthful members of the community. In the old days, it was the custom for local parishes to engage each other in this game, and according to one tradition, the prize, a keg of "genuine mountain dew" was attractive, for Highland whisky was appreciated no less than today. Shinty is a fine free game, much less restricted by rules but otherwise not unlike hockey which is derived from it. In old times, a field of shinty must have resembled a battleground; its usual accompaniment being skirling pipes and waving banners. Today the pipes still play a picturesque part, marching their teams on to the field of play and hailing their victories with piercing blasts of triumph.

Football

In England，all boys are taught at least one of the two kinds of football：soccer and rugger. In soccer，the ball cannot be touched with the hands or arms，but must be driven forward by kicking or by striking it with the body. This is the football usually played at day schools. Rugger is more like American football than is soccer；it is the kind most often played in boarding schools.

George Orwell（1903—1950）：He was an English writer. His work is marked by a profound consciousness of social injustice，an intense dislike of totalitarianism，and a passion for clarity in language. Considered "perhaps the 20th century's best chronicler of English culture"，he wrote works in many different genres including fiction，polemics，journalism，memoir and critical essays. His most famous works are two novels：*Animal Farm*（1945）and *Nineteen Eighty-Four*（1949）.

Movies to see

Seabiscuit—True story of the undersized Depression-era racehorse whose victories lifted not only the spirits of the team behind it but also those of the nation as well.

Victory—As allied POWs prepare for a soccer game against the German National Team to be played in Nazi-occupied Paris，the French Resistance and British officers are making plans for the team's escape.

Unit 12

Theatre and Music in the U.K.

> My idea is that there is music in the air, music all around us; the world is full of it, and you simply take as much as you require.
>
> —Edward Elgar
>
> I regard the theatre as the greatest of all art forms, the most immediate way in which a human being can share with another the sense of what it is to be a human being.
>
> —Oscar Wilde

Unit Goals

- To have a general view of British theatre and music
- To get acquainted with some great figures in the history of British theatre and music
- To develop critical thinking and intercultural communication skills
- To learn useful words and expressions concerning theatre and music in the U.K. and improve English language skills

Before You Read

Each of the following idioms is connected with the theatre.

1. Match the idioms with their definitions.

1) waiting in the wings	A. Good Luck! (said to somebody who is about to perform)
2) the show must go on	B. at the end of a show, the actors bow to the sounds of applause
3) in the spotlight	C. being ready and prepared to step into the action
4) to upstage somebody	D. being the focus of attention
5) break a leg	E. It is necessary to continue despite problems or difficulties
6) curtain call	F. to perform better than another person

2. Now complete the sentences by using one of the idioms above.

1) Before you perform Shakespeare's *Macbeth*, I'd just like to say that I hope you _____.

2) —We are having problems with our staff at the moment. Nearly half of them are off work with the flu.

—Well, I know it's difficult but _____. We can't just give up.

3) My boss is very angry with me, because I _____ him at the meeting. My ideas were much better received than his.

4) You should always do your best in your job because there are always people _____ to take your job if you don't do it well.

5) Go up and take a _____; your performance was fabulous.

6) I really like being _____; I find all the attention flattering.

Start to Read

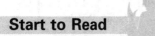
Text A　　　**Theatre and Music in the U.K.**

West End Shows

1 For many people，the **highlight** of a visit to London is the chance to see a West End show.

2 The West End of London，situated a stone's throw from Piccadilly Circus and Chinatown，is home to dozens of beautiful theatres.

3 London's West End theatres are **currently** enjoying a **boom** in popularity and ticket sales. According to the Society of London Theatres，nearly 12 million people attended a West End show last year，whilst audience numbers in 2005 **outstriped** that **impressive** figure.

4 One possible reason for the success of **contemporary theatrical** productions is the casting of **A-list** Hollywood actors in lead roles. Val Kilmer，star of films like *Top Gun* and *Batman Forever*，is currently appearing in *The Postman Always Rings Twice*.

5 And he is not alone—other American movie stars performing in London include Oscar winner，Kevin Spacey，and David Schwimmer，who found international fame in the **hit** TV **sitcom**，*Friends*.

6 British screen stars are also **treading** the boards in West End shows. Scottish actor，Ewan McGregor，is appearing in the **classic** 1950s **musical** *Guys and*

Dolls—an experience very different to making movies. McGregor says, "The actual process of making films is extraordinarily **tedious**. It is very difficult to keep your energy and focus, whereas what is wonderful about this is we have to create it together."

7 **Ironically**, it is not just that film stars are acting in plays nowadays but films themselves are being **adapted** for the stage. Amongst the films that can now be seen as plays or musicals are *The Lion King*, *A Few Good Men*, and *Billy Elliot*.

8 The longest-running shows in the West End are usually musicals. The Andrew Lloyd Webber show, *Cats*, ran for 21 years and 7000 performances, making its **composer** a **multi-millionaire**.

9 However, not all musicals do so well. *Oscar Wilde*: *The Musical* ran for only one night, closing after terrible reviews and poor bookings. It was quite possibly the biggest **flop** in London theatrical history.

Music in the U.K.

10 Have you ever heard of Al Martino? Not many people know his name nowadays, but back in 1952 he made history by becoming the first recording artist to have a number one record with his song "Here in My Heart."

11 For more than fifty years, sales of **singles** have been measured on a weekly basis and **ranked** in a chart. The week's **best-selling** single takes the number one position for that week.

12 So who has had the most number ones? For 25 years, the Beatles and Elvis Presley **matched** each other with 18 number one records apiece. However, in 2005, Elvis earned a **posthumous** number one when his 1957 hit "Jailhouse Rock" was re-released. Since then, two more Elvis singles have gone to the top of the charts bringing his total to 21 number ones!

13 Over the years, many artists have enjoyed **incredible** success in the charts. Bryan Adams held the number one position for 16 weeks in 1991 with the **ballad** "Everything I Do, I Do It for You" whilst Elton John's **tribute** to Princess Diana, "Candle in the Wind 97," sold 4.86 million copies in the U.K.

14 However, there are concerns over the future of the music industry as sales have fallen in recent years. This was **illustrated** in 2004 when Eric Prydz had a number one record despite having sold less than 24,000 copies.

15 One reason for the fall in CD sales could be the increase in music **downloads**. Many computer users **illegally** download MP3 **files** through peer-to-peer, file-sharing networks.

16 The music industry has **responded** to this new threat by offering the possibility to buy downloads from approved web sites. These **digital** downloads were **integrated** into the U.K. chart for the first time in April 2005. Ironically, the first number one of the digital age was a **re-issue** of Tony Christie's "Amarillo," a song first released in 1971.

After You Read

Knowledge Focus

1. **Mark the following statements with T if it is true or F if it is false.**

   1) West End of London is located not very far from Chinatown. _____

   2) Ticket sales for West End shows have been very poor in recent years due to high prices. _____

   3) Some American movie stars also perform in London's West End. _____

   4) The actor, Ewan McGregor, feels that the process of shooting a film is actually very boring. _____

   5) Many successful West End shows are adapted for the big screen and made into movies. _____

   6) Some West End musical can have a run lasting decades. _____

2. **Match the following songs with the correspondent singers.**

1) "Here in My Heart"	A. Elvis Presley
2) "Jailhouse Rock"	B. Bryan Adams
3) "Everything I Do, I Do It for You"	C. Al Martino
4) "Candle in the Wind"	D. Tony Christie
5) "Amarillo"	E. Elton John

Language Focus

1. **Mark the correct answer with a tick that means the same as the one quoted from the reading.**

   1) London's West End theatres are *currently* enjoying a boom in popularity and ticket sales.

      a) at present   b) for some time

   2) Audience numbers in 2005 look set to *outstrip* that impressive figure.

      a) be more important than   b) do better than

3) The actual process of making films is extraordinarily *tedious*. It is very difficult to keep your energy and focus.
   a) interesting but time-consuming　　　b) long and boring
4) It was quite possibly the biggest *flop* in London theatrical history.
   a) failure　　　　　　　　　　　　b) success
5) This was *illustrated* in 2004 when Eric Prydz had a number one record despite having sold less than 24,000 copies.
   a) explained by giving related examples　b) proven to be wrong

2. **Make the right choice to complete the sentence.**
   1) One possible reason for the success of contemporary theatrical productions is the casting of *A-list* Hollywood actors in lead roles; therefore, the success is partially because the actors _____.
      a) enjoy great popularity and fame　　b) are good at acting
   2) David Schwimmer found international fame in the *hit TV* sitcom, "Friends" and in fact the sitcom _____.
      a) is quite a disappointment　　　　b) is very successful
   3) In 2005, Elvis earned a *posthumous* number one when his 1957 hit "Jailhouse Rock" was re-released; it is both a pity and comfort that this success was achieved _____.
      a) after his death　　　　　　　　b) after many decades
   4) For 25 years, the Beatles and Elvis Presley *matched* each other with 18 number one records apiece; many people think their songs _____.
      a) enjoy almost equal popularity　　b) are out of date

3. **Complete the following sentences with the words given in proper forms.**
   1) There was something _____ (impression) about Julia's quiet dignity.
   2) It's _____ (legal) to carry guns in our country.
   3) That's the most _____ (credible) coincidence I've ever heard of!
   4) She works in a _____ (theatre) company and maybe she can get the tickets for us.
   5) _____ (irony), the murderer was killed with his own gun.
   6) The longest-running shows in the West End are usually _____ (music), and among them, *Cats* remains a big success.

4. **Proofreading and error correction.**
   The passage contains FIVE errors. Each indicated line contains a maximum of ONE error. In each case, only ONE word is involved.

The legacy of mainstream theatre in 1980s is the musical, a form imported from the USA but reinvented in Britain by Andrew Lloyd Webber, which string of successful shows (*Cats*, *Starlight Express*, *Phantom of the Opera*) make a substantial contribution to the economy. These shows rely on the spectacle of huge casts and technical wizardry, and their emphasis on escapist entertainment place them in the category of "populist culture". Webber's directing associate Trevor Nunn put the National back on its financial feet with *Les Misérables* in 1985, a musical adaptation of Hugo's novel, it continues touring internationally. Adaptation has become significant growth area in theatre as well as film and television, in an attempt to woo back audiences to the theatre.

1) _____

2) _____

3) _____

4) _____

5) _____

Comprehensive Work

1. **Team work**: **Choose one student of the team to present the story about one of the following Chinese idioms in English and other team members mime the story out.**
   ① His Spear Against His Shield ② Aping the Beauty
   ③ Making his Mark ④ The Vigil by the Tree Stump
   ⑤ Draw a Snake and Add Feet to It

2. **Role Play**: **Work in groups and present a mini-play based on the following story and students may make an adaptation of the story for the play.**

   In the reign of Emperor the Second of the Qin Dynasty (221 B.C. —207 B.C.), the prime minister Zhao Gao, obsessed with ambitions, was planning to usurp the throne day and night. But he did not know how many of the ministers in the court were allowed to be ordered about by him and how many of them were his opponents. So he thought out a way to test how high his prestige among the ministers was and also to find out who dared to oppose him.

   One day when court was held, Zhao Gao let someone bring a stag to the court and, with a broad smile on his face, he said to Emperor the Second of the Qin Dynasty, "Your Majesty, here is a fine horse I'm presenting to you."

   Looking at the animal, Emperor the Second thought that it was obviously a stag and that it could not be a horse. So he said smilingly to Zhao Gao, "My Prime Minister, you are wrong. This is a stag. Why do you say it is a horse?"

   Remaining calm, Zhao Gao said, "Will Your Majesty please see more clearly? This really is a horse that covers a thousand miles a day."

   Filled with suspicion, Emperor the Second looked at the stag again and said, "How can the antlers be grown on the head of a horse?"

Turning around and pointing his finger at the ministers, Zhao Gao said in a loud voice, "If Your Majesty do not believe me, you can ask the ministers."

The nonsense of Zhao Gao made the ministers totally at a loss, and they whispered to themselves, "What tricks was Zhao Gao playing? Was it not obvious that it was a stag?" But when they saw the sinister smile on Zhao Gao's face and his two rolling eyes gazing at each of them, they suddenly understood his evil intentions.

Some of the ministers who were timid and yet had a sense of righteousness did not dare to say anything, because to tell lies would make themselves uneasy and to tell the truth would mean that they would be persecuted by Zhao Gao later. Some ministers with a sense of justice persisted that it was a stag and not a horse. There were still some crafty and fawning ministers who followed Zhao Gao closely in ordinary times who immediately voiced their support to Zhao Gao, saying to the emperor, "This really is a horse that covers a thousand miles a day."

After the event, Zhao Gao punished by various means those ministers with a sense of justice who were not obedient to him, even with whole families of some of those ministers executed.

This story appears in *The Historical Records* written by Sima Qian. From this story people have derived the set phrase "calling a stag a horse" to mean deliberately misrepresenting something and misleading the public.

3. Essay Writing

Write a passage of about 300 words, presenting your understanding of the following question.

❖ What do you think might be the reasons that make West End shows so appealing?

Read More

Text B   **Pantomimes**

Read the following passage and finish the following exercises.

1) Most theatres in the country and a few London theatres put _____ (on/up) shows for children at _____ (Easter/Christmas) and many theatres have a theatre-in-education team working there.

2) Which of the following statements about Pantomime is NOT true? _____

a. Pantomime is a special kind of Christmas show for children.

b. Pantomime is loved by people of all ages and also allows the audience to join in.

c. "Pantomime" was the name of a Roman city.

d. A pantomime is always based on a well-known children's story.

3) A pantomime usually includes the following characters EXCEPT _____.

a. a principal boy   b. a clown   c. a dame   d. a horse

In many towns, an interest in the theatre is encouraged at a young age. Most theatres in the country and a few London theatres put on shows for children at Christmas and many theatres have a theatre-in-education team working there. This team, made up of actors and teachers, writes plays for children, usually performing them in the schools. They do different plays for different age groups and the children often take part in the play in some way. The children may take part by helping a character make a decision or they may have to warn a character about some kind of danger, perhaps by shouting a special word. Sometimes they even do some acting.

Pantomime is a special kind of Christmas show for children which is loved by people of all ages and which also allows the audience to join in. "Pantomime" was the name of the Roman actor who performed shows without speaking—this is where the English word "mime" comes from.

A pantomime is always based on a well-known children's story such as *Puss in Boots*, *Jack and the Beanstalk*, *Dick Whittington* or *Babies in the Wood*. But there are always certain types of characters in the show and certain situations and events. For example, a pantomime must always include a hero, known as the "principal boy" and this principal boy is always played by a pretty girl wearing a short costume. Then there is the comic older woman, known as the "dame," who is played by a man. There is always a chorus of young men and women who sing and dance and often there is a pantomime horse. The horse is played by two men who form the "front" and "back" ends inside a "horse" costume. It is funny and sometimes bad horse and it usually kicks the dame when she is not looking.

As well as the story which is being acted, a pantomime contains lots of songs, dances and comedy. Members of the audience have to shout a warning to one of the characters and argue with the character (usually the dame) when she does not believe them. When she shouts: "Oh no it isn't," the audience always responds with: "Oh yes it is!" The audience also learns and sings a simple song and a few children are sometimes invited onto the stage to help one of the characters during the show.

Text C　　Commercial Theatre and the Musical

Read the following passage and finish thefollowing exercises.

1) Which of the following statements about the musical is NOT true?

    a. The modern international musical originated in the West End.

    b. The musical was the most visible symbol of the commodification of British theatre.

c. The specific subject or story of the musical is the main source of the genre's appeal.

2) Lloyd Webber has produced all of the following musicals EXCEPT _____.

   a. *Phantom of the Opera*   b. *Cats*   c. *My Fair Lady*

3) The impact of the West End musical was politically conservative, because all of the following EXCEPT _____.

   a. the form privileged effect above content

   b. the prevailing tone is a concern with, contemporary political issues

   c. the real excitement comes from watching pure command of theatrical effect

One part of British theatre primed for the new language and priorities of monetarism was the commercial theatre, much of which thrived in the period, although in a very particular genre: the modern international musical. This phenomenon, originating in the West End, was the most visible symbol of the commodification of British theatre, and its commercial success was astonishing. British musicals were seen around the world, dominating the major theatre centres of many capital cities, including Broadway. The phenomenon was initially a handful of extraordinarily omnipresent productions, typified by the shows of composer-producer Andrew Lloyd Webber. More than any other development in the theatre since 1979, the success of the musical was an example of the transformation of the means of cultural production in the global marketplace.

Labour-intensive, often subject to high rents and with a product that cannot be "reproduced" indefinitely to achieve economies of scale, theatre has often required patronage, public and private, because it seemed a poor commercial prospect. Lloyd Webber, Cameron Mackintosh and others—like Wilson Barrett in the 1890s—demonstrated how the theatre could overcome its traditional economic constraints, this time by mounting several productions of the same show, opening simultaneously in global cities, accompanied by the aggressive marketing of both the show and its spin-off merchandising to increase profitability. These musicals stimulated demand to the point where their longevity, based on guaranteed audiences, was unique in the post-war period. The statistics are impressive. Lloyd Webber's *Cats*, for example, was originally produced (1981) with the financial backing of two hundred investors, some putting in as little as £1,000 each to produce the £450,000 cost of staging the show: by 1994, the investors were rewarded with annual profits of 200 per cent of their original investment. By 1992 *Cats* had grossed more than Steven Spielberg's *ET*, which was at the time the most profitable film ever made. By 1999 Lloyd Webber's *Phantom of the Opera* had grossed twice as much worldwide as James Cameron's film *Titanic* (1998). Newspaper listings on any day in this period indicated just how central musicals had become to the internationally oriented, tourist-driven metropolitan theatre culture. Of the forty-six London productions listed in the *Guardian* in August 2001, twenty-two were musicals, including *The Lion King*, *My Fair Lady* and *The Witches of Eastwick*, occupying some of the West End's largest theatres (the Lyceum, Drury Lane and the Prince of Wales, respectively). And there were many more musicals about to open, making the first year of the new millennium in this respect an unprecedented one.

Politically, the impact of the West End musical was conservative, largely because the form privileged effect above content. As John Bull has noted: "The prevailing tone is one of social irrelevance, of an unwillingness to discuss, or an unconcern with, contemporary political issues." Instead, it provided audiences with high production values and spectacle, a "conspicuous consumption" that, irrespective of the specific subject or story of particular shows, was the main source of the genre's appeal. Spectacle of this sort has an ideological impact, since it celebrates absorption over reflection, the impact of the signifier over what it might signify.

The ideology of the "spectacular" was particularly apparent in musicals that had an ostensible "content." *Les Misérables* was a case in point. Produced initially at the RSC's London home, the Barbican, in October 1985, the show transferred—by prior arrangement—to the Palace Theatre in December that year. The popular appeal of *Les Misérables* was undeniable, and it was still running in the early years of the twenty-first century. But the critical response was less enthusiastic and raised important issues, not least of which was the appropriateness of a major subsidised theatre using its resources to mount a show that could have been produced entirely commercially. One consistent criticism was, indeed, that spectacle triumphed over content. Hugo's novel is an impassioned critique of poverty, but, as Suzie Mackenzie commented in *Time Out*: "You are not asked to like *Les Misérables*. You are asked to admire it... on the grounds of melodrama, connivance and artifice... We are arrested by the spectacle of what we see, not moved by the pain of human suffering." Or as Michael Billington argued in the *Guardian*, "what you will remember is the spectacle, not the spiritual conflict... The real excitement comes from watching pure command of theatrical effect."

Text D The Beatles

Read the following passage and finish the following exercises.

1) _____ signaled the end of an era. The faint hope that one day the Beatles might get together again had gone forever.

2) George Harrison, John Lennon, Paul McCartney, and Ringo Starr formed the Beatles in _____ in 1960.
   a. Hamburg   b. New York   c. Liverpool

3) At first, the themes of the Beatles were precisely those that occupied and concerned their young audience; later, they reflected the climate of the 1960s and sang of social _____ and political _____.

4) What is it that made the Beatles special? State the reasons based on the following passage.
   ① _____
   ② _____
   ③ _____

When John Lennon was murdered in 1980 outside his New York apartment by a young man for whom he had earlier autographed a record cover, it signaled the end of an era. The faint hope that one day the Beatles might get together again had gone forever, but, more importantly, gone were the optimism that they represented and the social consciousness that they spread.

George Harrison, John Lennon, Paul McCartney, and Ringo Starr formed the Beatles in Liverpool in 1960. Harrison, Lennon, and McCartney had gained experience playing at a club in Hamburg, Germany, but it was at the Cavern, in Liverpool, their home city, that the Beatles' career really began to take off.

Their first single record, "Love Me Do," was released in October 1962. Four months later, their second, "Please, Please Me," went straight into the top ten and soon reached the coveted number one spot, while their first LP became the fastest-selling long-playing record of 1963. Although the group broke up, millionaires all, in 1970, their records still sell over the world. What is it that made the Beatles special?

As a group they were competent, and their voices were pleasant, but this would not have been enough. They were probably lucky in their influences: the colorful Merseyside environment from which they sprang, combined with an admiration for Afro-American rhythm-and-blues also, they were fortunate in the rapport that they found with one another and with their audience while the songwriting partnership of Lennon and McCartney produced a stream of brilliant hits.

At first, their themes were precisely those that occupied and concerned their young audience: love, sorrow, good luck, bad luck, and the quaint characters that are always to be found in any big city. Later, they reflected the climate of the 1960s and sang of social inequality and political injustice. In addition, they created melodies that were rich and original enough to be played and sung by musicians of the caliber of Count Basie and Ella Fitzgerald.

The Beatles were special because they believed in their own talents. They copied no one, and they were strong enough not to allow themselves to be destroyed by the overnight achievement of success beyond the reach of the imagination. In this they probably owed much to their record producer, George Martin, and their manager, Brian Epstein. The Beatles were also special because they were a strong positive force in a time of great social and political disenchantment. They were a voice for the young people of the time.

Notes

1. **Edward Elgar** (1857—1934): He was an English composer. Several of his first major orchestral works, including the *Enigma Variations* and the *Pomp and Circumstance Marches*, were greeted with acclaim. He also composed oratorios, chamber music, symphonies, instrumental concertos, and songs. He was appointed Master of the King's Musick in 1924.

2. Oscar Wilde (1854—1900): He was an Irish playwright, poet and author of numerous short stories and one novel. Known for his biting wit, he became one of the most successful playwrights of the late Victorian era in London, and one of the greatest celebrities of his day. Several of his plays continue to be widely performed, especially *The Importance of Being Earnest*.

For Fun

Movies to see

Billy Elliot—A talented young boy becomes torn between his unexpected love of dance and the disintegration of his family.

Music and Lyrics—A washed up singer is given a couple days to compose a chart-topping hit for an aspiring teen sensation. Though he's never written a decent lyric in his life, he sparks with an offbeat younger woman with a flair for words.

Songs to enjoy

Memory by Sarah Brightman—Midnight, not a sound from the pavement / Has the moon lost her memory / She is smiling alone...

Yesterday by the Beatles—Yesterday, all my troubles seemed so far away / Now it looks as though they're here to stay / Oh, I believe in yesterday...

Unit 13

The British Holidays and Festivals

> Working hours are never long enough. Each day is a holiday, and ordinary holidays are grudges as enforced interruptions in an absorbing vocation.
>
> —Winston Churchill
>
> If all the year were playing holidays, to sport would be as tedious as to work.
>
> —William Shakespeare

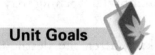

Unit Goals

- To get to know some traditional British holidays and festivals
- To learn the British traditions and customs related to the holidays and festivals
- To develop critical thinking and intercultural communication skills
- To learn useful words and expressions concerning British holidays and festivals and improve English language skills

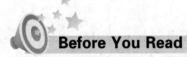

Before You Read

1. **Work with your partner and share ideas with each other.**
   1) How do you understand the quotes above? Are holidays necessary or not? How do you usually spend holidays?
   2) What is the importance of observing traditional festivals?

2. **Match the following symbols with the festivals.**
   ① carnations   ② Santa Claus   ③ bunny and eggs
   ④ roses   ⑤ pumpkins

   _____ [   ] (February 14)
   _____ [   ] (A Sunday between March 22 and April 25)

_____ 〔   〕(the second Sunday in May)
_____ 〔   〕(October 31)
_____ 〔   〕(December 25)

Start to Read

Text A   Holidays and Festivals in the U.K.

1 The British Calendar is full of holidays and festivals which **demonstrate** the different cultures and histories of the people who make up Britain.

England

2 November 5, Guy Fawkes Day, is an English holiday celebrating the **preservation** of the British monarchy and Parliament. Guy Fawkes was one of the 13 **conspirators** who planned a gunpowder **explosion** aimed at killing King James I and the members of Parliament on the assembly's opening day, November 5, 1605.

3 By the time James I became king after the death of Queen Elizabeth I in 1603, English **Catholics** were tired of the harsh treatment they had been receiving under Queen Elizabeth I. Catholics who refused to attend **Protestant** church services were heavily **penalized**. These Catholics, called **recusants**, were fined, could not be married or **baptized** according to Catholic rites, and could not employ Catholic servants or schoolmates. Anyone failing to follow the rules could be **imprison**ed.

4 When James I took the throne, English Catholics hoped this treatment would end. However, **persecution** of Catholics continued under James, and the Catholics became **desperate** for a solution.

5 **Consequently**, thirteen Catholic men developed a **drastic** plot. They hoped to rid the country of James and all Parliament members and put a Catholic monarch in James' place. James' nine-year-old daughter Elizabeth, although Protestant, was thought to be **pliable** enough to be converted to Catholicism, and thus became a focus of the conspirators' plot.

6 The conspirators **smuggled** 36 barrels of gunpowder into the cellar of Parliament, intending to blow up the building. Fortunately for James, an **anonymous** letter **alerted** him to the danger and he had the cellar watched.

When Fawkes arrived to **ignite** the powder, he was caught and **tortured** until he **revealed** the names of his fellow plotters, all of whom were later **captured**. Parliament then declared the fifth of November to be "a holiday forever, in thankfulness to God for our deliverance."

7 English children today celebrate Guy Fawkes Day by making huge rag dolls called "guys" and calling out, "A penny for the guy?" to passersby. The money collected is used to buy fireworks, which are set off on the night of the fifth. The English also light huge bonfires and toss the rag "guys" into the flames. That day, throughout England, people **chant**:

8 Remember, remember the fifth of November,

Gunpowder treason and plot.

We see no reason

why gunpowder **treason**

Should ever be forgot!

Scotland

9 While most British people welcome the coming of the New Year with parties, in Scotland, New Year's Eve called **Hogmanay**, is the major winter celebration, and **overshadows** Christmas which is a very quiet affair.

10 How Hogmanay is celebrated varies throughout Scotland, but one widely practiced custom is "first footing." The custom in the early hours of January 1st is still kept up with great **vigor**. There is a **superstitious** belief that the first person to cross the **threshold** of a household can bring luck and **prosperity**. The First Foot comes as soon as possible after midnight has struck. He brings symbolic gifts of food or fuel or money as **tokens** of prosperity. Sometimes, instead of these presents, or in addition to them, he carries a bunch of evergreens as a promise of continuing life. In return, the luck-bringer must be **hospitably** entertained with food and plentiful supplies of wine or spirits as his reward.

11 To be a true luck-bringer, the First Foot should be **vigorous** and healthy and, if possible, young and good-looking. If he is flat-footed, or cross-eyed, or lame, if his eyebrows meet across his nose, if he is dressed in black, or appears to be **ailing**, the **omens** for the coming twelve months are bad. In most areas, the appearance

of a young, preferably dark-haired and handsome man, is considered particularly lucky.

12 Each year Scottish people all over the world also celebrate their most beloved national poet, Robert Burns, by holding a Burns Supper on the evening of his birthday (25th January). Burns wrote mainly in the Scots **dialect** and his poems drew on older traditions of Scottish folk songs and stories and they have a wide popular **appeal**.

Northern Ireland

13 Northern Irish Catholics celebrate the birthday of the patron saint of Ireland, St. Patrick, on March 17 each year. Patrick was a Catholic **bishop**

who lived in the 5th century and is thought to have brought Christianity to Ireland. He lived in Great Britain, but at the age of 16, he was captured by Irish **raiders**, taken to Ireland and made a slave. He **eventually** escaped and returned to Britain, where he had a dream in which the Irish begged him to return. Although his memories of years of slavery in Ireland made him hesitate, he followed this call and had a very successful **missionary** career.

14 According to popular legend, St. Patrick drove snakes (the Christian symbol of evil) out of Ireland. In another legend, it is said that he used the three leafed **clover**, or **shamrock**, to explain the Christian **trinity** (Father, Son and Holy Ghost) to the **pagan** Irish. The shamrock is a popular symbol to wear on St. Patrick's Day, and it is also considered very lucky to wear something green.

Wales

15 Wales has some of the oldest and richest **literary**, musical and poetic traditions in Europe. Poems written in the traditional Welsh language and style are governed by ancient codes and conventions which can be traced back to the Druids, who **instituted** **rigid** rules of **composition** to help them to correctly memorise and pass on poems and stories. In pre-14th century Wales, to become a **bard** or **harper** required years of study and was considered a profession, like law or medicine.

16 This poetic tradition has been celebrated for centuries in Eisteddfod, a Welsh word meaning a gathering where people **recite** verses and sing songs. In 1536, Wales was officially joined with England and English became the national language. Speaking Welsh was seen as a bad thing. As recently as the 19th century, Welsh schoolchildren could be punished for speaking Welsh.

The Welsh language began to die, but Welsh speakers fought hard to **preserve** it. One way they accomplished this was to celebrate their culture and their language each August with a really large Eisteddfod which would remind people throughout the U.K. of Wales' special cultural heritage. The Eisteddfod is now the largest popular festival of music making and poetry writing in Europe.

17 At the Eisteddfod, tents and **pavilions** are erected around a big open space: in the different tents competitions are held to find the best **choirs**, translators, **essayists** and poets. The **highlight** is the **crowning** of the two bards who have written the best poems of the festival.

After You Read

Knowledge Focus

1. **Match the holidays or festivals with the places.**

Hogmanay	England
Eisteddfod	Scotland
St. Patrick's Day	Wales
Guy Fawkes Day	Northern Ireland
Burns Night	

2. **Sort the symbols and customs under the correspondent festivals or holidays.**

   ① rag dolls   ② shamrock   ③ evergreens
   ④ first footing   ⑤ bards and poetry   ⑥ dark-haired man
   ⑦ tents and pavilions ⑧ green dress   ⑨ bonfire

Guy Fawkes Day	Eisteddfod	Hogmanay	St. Patrick's Day

Language Focus

1. **Complete the following sentences with proper words.**

capture	preserve	overshadow	alert	appeal
highlight	smuggle	desperate	anonymous	

1) As a mother of three children, she is _____ for work.

2) The city should take steps to _____ the ancient building.

3) Their daring escape has _____ the imagination of the whole country.

4) The Disaster Fund received a (an) _____ donation of $ 5000.

5) A campaign was launched to _____ the public to the dangers of smoking.

6) He managed to _____ a message out of prison to his friends.

7) Films of that sort have lost their _____ for me.

8) Her new book will _____ all her earlier ones.

9) Recorded _____ of today's big football game will be shown after the news.

2. **Fill in each blank with a suitable preposition or adverb.**

1) The British Calendar is full of holidays and festivals which demonstrate the different cultures and histories of the people who make _____ Britain.

2) Guy Fawkes was one of the 13 conspirators who planned a gunpowder explosion aimed _____ killing King James I and the members of Parliament.

3) English Catholics were tired _____ the harsh treatment they had been receiving _____ Queen Elizabeth I.

4) Persecution of Catholics continued _____ James, and the Catholics became desperate _____ a solution.

5) They hoped to rid the country _____ James and all Parliament members and put a Catholic monarch _____ James' place.

6) Fortunately for James, an anonymous letter alerted him _____ the danger and he had the cellar watched.

7) _____ return, the luck-bringer must be hospitably entertained _____ food and plentiful supplies of wine or spirits as his reward.

8) They celebrate their culture and their language each August _____ a really large Eisteddfod which would remind people throughout the U. K. _____ Wales' special cultural heritage.

3. **Fill in the blanks with the proper form of the words in the brackets.**

1) The aim of the policy is the _____ (preserve) of peace.

2) After the _____ (explode), it was some time before the town resumed its everyday routines.

3) He revealed their _____ (conspire) to overthrow the government.

4) Many coal-miners were _____ (prison) in a pit accident.

5) They came to America after being _____ (persecution) for their religious beliefs.

6) It's a common _____ (superstitious) that black cats are unlucky.

7) The new government ushered in a period of _____ (prosperous).

8) Though nearly 50, he was exceptionally _____ (vigor) in work.

4. Proofreading and error correction.

The passage contains FIVE errors. Each indicated line contains a maximum of ONE error. In each case, only ONE word is involved.

One reason that Hogmanay has become such a jubilant celebration may due to the fact that Christmas celebrations were essentially banned in Scotland for nearly 400 years—since the end of the 17th century to the 1950s. During a period of religious upheaval known as the Protestant Reformation, the Protestant Church in Scotland decided that people have gotten too far away from the most important elements of their religion. They wanted to "purify" their church and also to separate from anything might be considered Catholic, so they banned Christmas celebrations. Many Scots had to work during Christmas, therefore New Year became the time to celebrate the winter solstice, hold parties, and exchange gifts with family and friends.	1) _____ 2) _____ 3) _____ 4) _____ 5) _____

Comprehensive Work

1. Group Work: Work in groups of four and share ideas with group members.

Nowadays, more and more people are developing a craving for traveling.

Discuss with your group members, what might be the motives for the traveling fever?

1. _____
2. _____
3. _____
4. _____
   ...

2. Essay Writing

Write a passage of about 300 words, presenting your understanding of the following questions.

❖ Is it all right for the Chinese people to observe western festivals?

❖ Why or why not?

Read More

Text B Holiday Life in England

Read the following passage and finish the following exercises.

1) It is a day when stores launch one of the year's biggest sales periods. In the U. K. , it is traditionally a day for sporting activity, originally fox hunting. The holiday mentioned above is _____.

2) Which of the following statements about Easter is NOT correct? _____
   A. It used to be the day on which the ladies would parade in the parks, wearing new dresses and hats.
   B. It is generally regarded as an unofficial consecration of Spring.
   C. It is common to spend the day with family members or friends as a sort of "second" Christmas Day.
   D. On Easter Monday, there are funfairs with roundabouts, coconut-shies, switchbacks and other amusements in many towns.

3) The August Bank Holiday is likely to cause traffic congestion. The statement is _____. (true/ false)

In England, Christmas Day and Good Friday have been holidays (literally "Holy Days") for religious reasons since the establishment of Christianity in this country. Christmas is celebrated on December 25, not Christmas Eve as in several other European countries.

Britain has relatively few public holidays compared with other European countries. They are usually described as Bank Holidays because they are days when banks are officially closed. The public holidays (or "Bank Holidays") are Easter Monday, May Day (May 1st), the Spring Bank Holiday (the last Monday in May), the Summer Bank Holiday (the last Monday in August), December 26th (Boxing Day), and New Year's Day.

Boxing Day is a holiday of particularly British origin. The holiday takes its name from the old custom of giving employees or tradesmen (such as the milkman) an annual present or "Christmas box" on that day, and it has nothing to do with the sport of "boxing". If Christmas day or Boxing Day falls at the weekend, the weekday which follows December 25th and 26th becomes a Bank Holiday. It is common to spend the day with family members or friends as a sort of "second" Christmas Day, where presents may be exchanged, the left-overs of the previous day are eaten or another family meal is prepared in celebration. It is also a day when stores launch one of the year's biggest sales periods. Boxing Day in the U. K. is traditionally a day for sporting activity, originally fox hunting, but as this is now banned, alternative hunts take place.

Easter Monday is generally regarded as an unofficial consecration of Spring. In many towns there are funfairs with roundabouts, coconut-shies, switchbacks and other amusements. The fair on Hampstead, Heath, in the north of London, is particularly famous. Easter Monday used to be the day on which the ladies would parade in the parks, wearing new dresses and hats. Although this custom is dying out, the tradition still provides the ladies with a pretext for buying spring clothes.

The August Bank Holiday is probably the most popular one of the year, partly because it comes at a time when children are not at school. Very many people try to make this a long weekend, and go away to seaside or the country. The result is that anyone who can manage to take a holiday at another time would be well advised to do so, for the roads get congested with traffic (in England, there are more vehicles per mile of road than in any other country).

Text C   Valentine Customs

Read the following passage and finish the following exercises.

1) Most cards are romantic and express love messages which do not let on who the sender is because the sender does not want to _____.
   a) reveal his true identity   b) hide his true identity

2) Most of the nasty cards were addressed to the pot-bellied, cross-eyed, one-legged or to old maids, wishing them the three dreadful "Ds": Disgrace, Death or _____.
   a) Disgust   b) Damnation

3) Anyone who reads the British national papers on 14 February will see messages for somene's Very Special Person. Unexpectedly, _____ has more columns of lovers' messages than any other paper.
   a) *The Times*   b) *The Guardian*

4) The British newspaper ad brigade tend to see themselves or the desired one as animals with _____ the firm favorites.
   a) fleas   b) bears

5) A girl can tell the occupation of her future husband by noting which bird she sees first on 14 February. But if it's a _____ she will find no man at all.
   a) raven   b) woodpecker

People in countries as far apart as Japan, the United States, Australia and France send Valentine cards to someone in Britain they fancy on 14 February, St. Valentine's Day. Most cards are romantic and express secret love messages which do not let on who the sender is.

There was a time in Victorian Britain when men used to send rude and insulting cards to tease a lady they either loved or loathed. The problem for the recipient was trying to guess not only who the sender was, but also what his secret feelings might be. Most of the nasty cards were addressed to the pot-bellied, cross-eyed, one-legged or to old maids, wishing them the three dreadful "Ds": Disgrace, Death or Damnation.

The lovesick British excel themselves each Valentine's Day by buying up huge spaces in newspapers to fill with messages for a Very Special Person. Anyone who reads the British national papers on 14 February will see romantic Britons at their most lovelorn, cryptic and erotic. Unexpectedly, *The Times* has more columns of lovers' messages than any other paper. Next is usually *The Daily Mail*, followed by *The Guardian*, *Daily Mirror*, *Daily Express* and *The Daily Telegraph*.

Senders of newspaper messages, whether they are in Britain, North America or Australia, must get a thrill out of their exhibitionism without letting on who is the secret admirer hidden in the words of the advertisement. The British newspaper ad brigade tend to see themselves or the desired one as animals, with bears the firm favorites. But fleas, toads, bugs and mice are well represented.

Food symbols often occur too: prunes and cookies are popular, also cherry pies and sausages. A lot of items are prefaced by "tasty", "crunchy" or "yummy".

Who is this saint whose fame has spread around the world? In truth, there are 52 St. Valentines, but no one knows which gave his name to Valentine's Day. One fact is acknowledged by love historians: all the likely candidates were martyred, dying with their knots of celibacy still securely tied. One Valentine gave aid to persecuted Christians, and while in prison for this he formed a friendship with the blind daughter of his gaoler. When he was taken away to be executed, he wrote her a farewell message, which he signed: "From your Valentine."

Whether or not this is the right Valentine, one thing is certain: the name Valentine means "powerful" or "strong".

In parts of the English countryside, it is still believed that a girl can tell the occupation of her future husband by noting which bird she sees first on 14 February.

But if it is a woodpecker she will find no man at all. Happy bird watching! Happy Valentine's Day!

For Fun

Movies to see

Twelfth Night: Or What You Will—Brother Sebastian and sister Viola, who are not only very close but look a great deal alike, are in a shipwreck, and both think the other dead...

The Holiday—Two women troubled with guy-problems swap homes in each other's countries, where they each meet a local guy and fall in love.

Unit 14
The British Literature (I)

> The books that the world calls immoral are the books that show the world its own shame.
>
> —Oscar Wilde
>
> A good novel tells us the truth about its hero; but a bad novel tells us the truth about its author.
>
> —G. K. Chesterton

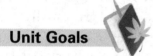

Unit Goals

- To have a general view of British literature
- To get acquainted with some famous British writers and works
- To develop critical thinking and intercultural communication skills
- To learn useful words and expressions concerning British literature and improve English language skills

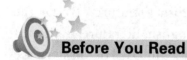

Before You Read

Test your knowledge on British literature. Match the storylines with the correspondent Shakespeare's plays.

① Prince of Denmark returns home to find his father murdered and his mother remarrying the murderer, his uncle. Meanwhile, war is brewing.

② Two couples fall in love with the wrong partners, and they are finally brought together rightly.

③ The King, old and tired, divides his kingdom among his daughters, giving great importance to their protestations of love for him.

④ A wicked guy convinces the General that his wife has been unfaithful.

⑤ When a merchant must default on a large loan from an abused Jewish moneylender for a friend with romantic ambitions, the bitterly vengeful creditor demands a gruesome

payment instead.

⑥ A ruthlessly ambitious Scottish lord seizes the throne with the help of his scheming wife and a trio of witches.

_____	_Macbeth_	_____	_A Midsummer Night's Dream_
_____	_Othello_	_____	_King Lear_
_____	_Hamlet_	_____	_The Merchant of Venice_

Start to Read

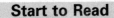

Text A **Overview of British Literature (I)**

Old English Literature

1 The study of English literature usually begins with the Anglo-Saxon epic poem _Beowulf_. It tells the story of the 6th century Swedish **warrior** Beowulf. The scene of _Beowulf_ is not England but Denmark. The poem tells how the great feasting hall of King Hrothgar, the Dane, is **raided** repeatedly by Grendel, a frightful sea **monster**. Beowulf comes from Sweden to aid Hrothgar. He slays Grendel and, in an undersea struggle, also kills Grendel's equally dangerous mother. In later years, Beowulf, king of his own land, dies in the act of killing a fire dragon that is **menacing** to his people.

Middle English Literature

2 With the Norman Conquest in 1066, Britain entered the Middle Ages (1066—1485). The Middle English period sees the true beginning of the

magnificent heritage of English literature. By far the greatest name in Middle English literature is that of Geoffrey Chaucer (1340? —1400). His **masterpiece** is _The Canterbury Tales_, which is made up of a series of stories told by **pilgrims** to entertain each other on their way to the tomb of Thomas Becket at Canterbury. _The Canterbury Tales_ is **notable** for its **diversity**, both in

the range of social types amongst the 31 pilgrims, and the range in style of the stories they tell. His people—the **knight**, nuns, priests, landowner, scholar, miller, housewife, farmer and many others—give a **cross-section** of **medieval** life.

Elizabethan Drama

3 There was a general **flowering** of cultural and intellectual life in Europe during the 15th and 16th centuries which is known as "The **Renaissance**." In British culture, one of the most successful and long-lasting expressions of this development lay in drama. The first professional theatre opened in London in 1576, and others followed, producing the works of many notable playwrights, including Christopher Marlow (1564—1593), Ben Jonson, and of course, William Shakespeare.

4 Marlow was the earliest of this great **trio**, and his style is thought to have had a great influence on Shakespeare. His most famous play is *Doctor Faustus*. It tells the story of a man who sells his soul to the Devil in return for power, knowledge and pleasure. The play **consequently** seems to teach a moral lesson in the fashion of the earlier **morality** plays, but also questions the limits placed on human knowledge by an apparently **vengeful** God.

"If music is the food of love ... I'm full."

5 Shakespeare was a man of the late Renaissance who gave the fullest expression to humanist ideals. He was born and died at Stratford-upon-Avon. He was in London an actor, poet and playwright. Shakespeare's plays fall into **categories**, or classes. He **excels** in each kind. The **tragedies** include *Romeo and Juliet*, *Hamlet*, *Othello*, *King Lear* and *Macbeth*. Among the **comedies** are *The Taming of the Shrew*, *A Midsummer Night's Dream*, *Twelfth Night* and *The*

Tempest. His history plays, based on English history, include *Richard III*, *Richard II*, *Henry IV* and *Henry V*. *Julius Caesar* and *Antony and Cleopatra* are tragedies on **classical themes**. Taken as a whole, it could be said that Shakespeare's early works showed **optimism** and his belief that love and **benevolence** will **triumph** over everything and concern for a peaceful and unified England whereas his later works, with deep **insight**, brought to light the contradiction between the **humanists** and the reality.

The 17th Century

6 The Essays of Francis Bacon (1561—1626) made popular in English a literary form widely practiced afterward. Bacon was a public figure and **statesman** of importance under both Elizabeth and James, rising to the high post of Lord Chancellor. A **scandal** ended his public

service in 1621. He devoted the rest of his life wholly to literature and scholarship. Bacon was a very learned man, and in his essays much of his learning is unloaded. He follows the correct essay method in choosing **miscellaneous** subjects, such as Friendship, Studies, Gardens, and so on. He treats his subjects with **vigour**, fluency, and a pleasant play of fancy and learning.

7 The literary giant of the 17th century, John Milton (1608—1674) was much bound up in Puritan Revolution. His literary talents showed themselves in early works. The twin poems "L'Allegro" and "Il Penseroso" present two different views of life—that of the lively man and that of the thoughtful man. Religious and political **disputes** also interested Milton, and he wrote many **pamphlets** on these subjects. Milton took the side of Parliament in the Civil War and wrote pamphlets supporting the king's **execution**. During the **protectorate**, he served as Latin secretary to Cromwell, composing many state documents in that language. When Charles II came to the throne in 1660, Milton's position was **endangered** and he was heavily fined. During his retirement from public life, he produced his masterpieces: the epic *Paradise Lost*, its sequel *Paradise Regained*, and the poetic tragedy *Samson Agonistes*.

The 18th Century

8 The course of the 18th century presents a broad contrast to the **disruption** and change of the 17th century. A desire for **rational** agreement and an increasing confidence is the **keynote** of the century.

9 Jonathan Swift (1667—1745), Irish-born, became a priest of the Church of Ireland and later dean of St. Patrick's **Cathedral** in Dublin. He spent a number of early years in England, and he was interested in English politics all his life. His name is linked with the fanciful **account** of four **voyages** known as *Gulliver's Travels*. By a series of extraordinary adventures, Gulliver, in return, visits giants, **pigmies**, crazy **philosophers**, and a race of horse-people.

10 Scotland produced a much-loved poet, Robert Burns (1759—1796), who wrote in Scottish **dialect**. Among the most cherished of his poems are "Holy Willie's Prayer," "To A Mouse," and "To A Louse." Among his songs are "Comin' thro' the Rye" and "Auld Lang Syne." He remains the best loved folk poet of Scotland.

11 Daniel Defoe (1660—1731) led an active life as a **journalist** and political pamphleteer. More than once his opinions carried him into prison. Defoe's first and greatest novel appeared in 1719. This was *Robinson Crusoe*, the most famous tale of **shipwreck** and **solitary** survival in all literature.

After You Read

Knowledge Focus

1. Match the following literary works with the correspondent storylines.

①　*Doctor Faustus*　　②　*Beowulf*
③　*Robinson Crusoe*　　④　*The Canterbury Tales*
⑤　*Gulliver's Travels*

1) It is made up of a series of stories told by pilgrims to entertain each other on their way to the tomb of St. Thomas Becket.
2) It tells the story of a man who sells his soul to the Devil in return for power, knowledge and pleasure.
3) It tells the story of the 6th century Swedish warrior.
4) It is about a series of extraordinary adventures involving giants, pigmies, crazy philosophers, and a race of horse-people.
5) It tells the most famous tale of shipwreck and solitary survival in all literature.

2. Sort the following plays into different categories.

1) *Antony and Cleopatra*　　2) *The Tempest*
3) *Othello*　　4) *Henry V*
5) *Macbeth*　　6) *The Taming of the Shrew*
7) *Richard II*　　8) *Twelfth Night*
9) *Hamlet*　　10) *Henry IV*
11) *A Midsummer Night's Dream*　　12) *King Lear*
13) *Julius Caesar*　　14) *Romeo and Juliet*
15) *Richard III*

A. Tragedies: _____
B. Comedies: _____
C. History Plays: _____

Language Focus

1. Complete the following sentences with proper words and expressions.

fall into	menacing	endanger	triumph over
benevolence	miscellaneous	cross-section	excel
flowering	notable	keynote	bring to light

1) The dark _____ clouds overhead suggest a coming storm and everyone is

making his way back home.

2) When their accounts were examined, several errors were _____.

3) This area is _____ for its pleasant climate.

4) Advancing culture is bound to _____ declining culture.

5) When it comes to singing, she really _____.

6) His _____ made it possible for many poor children to attend college.

7) The lecture series _____ naturally _____ three parts.

8) A small boy's pockets are likely to contain a _____ collection of objects.

9) Unemployment has been the _____ of the conference.

10) You will _____ your health if you work so hard.

11) The research interviewed a _____ of the American public.

12) Many would say the Renaissance saw the finest _____ of European culture.

2. **Complete the following sentences with the words given in proper forms.**

1) Most _____ (learn) men are modest.

2) We should get a thorough understanding about the cultural _____ (diverse) of the United States.

3) His intention was good, but his _____ (execute) of the plan was unsatisfactory.

4) According to some _____ (philosophy), everything in existence is reasonable.

5) I am unconcerned with questions of religion or _____ (moral).

6) He had been ill for a long time and _____ (consequence) he was behind in his work.

3. **Fill in each blank with a suitable preposition or adverb.**

1) In British culture one of the most successful and long-lasting expressions of this development lay _____ drama.

2) Marlow's style is thought to have had a great influence _____ Shakespeare.

3) It tells the story of a man who sells his soul to the Devil _____ return for power, knowledge and pleasure.

4) The play consequently seems to teach a moral lesson _____ the fashion of the earlier morality plays.

5) The play also questions the limits placed _____ human knowledge by an apparently vengeful God.

6) Shakespeare's plays fall _____ categories, or classes. He excels _____ each kind.

7) Shakespeare's early works showed his belief that love and benevolence will triumph _____ everything and concern _____ a peaceful and unified England.

8) The literary giant of the 17th century, John Milton was much bound _____ in Puritan Revolution.

9) A desire _____ rational agreement and an increasing confidence is the keynote of the century.

10) Bacon treats his subjects _____ vigour, fluency, and a pleasant play of fancy

and learning.

4. Proofreading and error correction.

The passage contains FIVE errors. Each indicated line contains a maximum of ONE error. In each case, only ONE word is involved.

Shakespeare's command of language, though overwhelming, is not unique and is incapable of imitation. Poetry written in English becomes Shakespearean frequently enough to testify the contaminating power of his high rhetoric. The peculiar magnificence of Shakespeare is in his power of representation of human character and personality and their mutabilities. The canonical praise of this magnificence inaugurated by Samuel Johnson's preface to the Shakespeare of 1765, and is both revelatory and misled: "Shakespeare is above all writers, at least above all modern writers, the poet of nature, the poet holds up to his readers a faithful mirror of manners and of life."

1) _____

2) _____

3) _____

4) _____

5) _____

Comprehensive Work

1. **Group Work: Work in groups and present a short story.**

   The rules:

   1) There are four groups of words and your story must include all the words from any group you've chosen.

   2) The story you are about to present must fall into a certain category that are given below.

   A. rumour, diamond, tiger, nap, thunderstorm, thief
   B. oasis, hero, diary, moon, balloon, stepmother
   C. headline, popcorn, rock, seashell, proposal, wolf
   D. singer, window, journey, camera, apartment, cat

   I. Children's   II. Crime   III. Romance   IV. Humor   V. Sci-fi

   Our team will choose Group (A. B. C. D) and Category (I, II, III, IV, V) to present a story.

2. **Essay Writing**

   Write a passage of about 300 words, presenting your understanding of the following questions.

   ❖ What is your favorite literary genre, drama, poetry or fiction?

   ❖ Why?

Read More

| Text B | William Shakespeare |

Read the following passage and finish the following exercises.

1) Shakespeare was born in Stratford-upon-Avon in _____ on April the 23rd and he wrote _____ plays and _____ sonnets.

2) Shakespeare's works look at common human themes, such as _____, murder, lust, power, _____ and love.

3) Shakespeare's influence on the English language can still be felt today. Choose the correct expressions to complete the following sentences.

　① fair play　　② much ado about nothing　　③ thin air

A. The contestants agreed to observe the spirit of _____ in all of the games.

B. We can't just produce another $1000 out of _____.

C. We can use _____ to describe a situation in which there has been a lot of excitement about something that is not really important.

Of all the famous English writers, probably the best known is William Shakespeare.

He was born in Stratford-upon-Avon in 1564 on April the 23rd. His father was an important man in town so Shakespeare had a good upbringing. Shakespeare probably went to school (although no records survive to prove this) but not university. He got married when he was 18 to Anne Hathaway and the couple had 3 children.

Shakespeare wrote 38 plays and 154 sonnets. He began working in his home town of Stratford but by 1592 was writing in London. He became rich enough to buy a house in the capital and one in Stratford.

He wrote sad stories called tragedies, like *Romeo and Juliet*, funny stories or comedies, romantic stories and stories about historical figures such as *Julius Caesar*.

Shakespeare died on his birthday in 1616, almost 400 years ago. But why is his work still popular today?

His work looked at common human themes, such as betrayal, murder, lust, power, ambition and love. These themes are as much a part of human nature today as they were all those years ago and are the themes we see in modern soap operas and Hollywood films. Even though his theatre, The Globe, burned down in 1613 it was rebuilt in London in 1997 and you can still see his plays performed there today.

Shakespeare's influence on the English language can still be felt today. We talk about "fair play," meaning honest behaviour but this phrase was first used by Shakespeare. He coined the phrase "you can have too much of a good thing." And it was Shakespeare who came up with the expression to disappear "into thin air" which we still use today when we lose something.

Shakespeare's work has been translated into every major language in the world. And perhaps we'll still be as fascinated by his work 400 years from now.

Text C   To Be, or Not to Be

Read the following passage and finish the following exercises.

1) The following passage is an excerpt from the work _____, which was written by _____.

2) The following passage is in fact a soliloquy by the hero _____.

3) "To be, or not to be: that is the question" can be interpreted as _____.

4) From the following passage, we can get some clues about the speaker's character. He seems to be _____.

To be, or not to be: that is the question:
Whether 'tis nobler in the mind to suffer
The slings and arrows of outrageous fortune,
Or to take arms against a sea of troubles,
And by opposing end them? To die: to sleep;
No more; and by a sleep to say we end
The heart-ache and the thousand natural shocks
That flesh is heir to, 'tis a consummation
Devoutly to be wish'd. To die, to sleep;
To sleep: perchance to dream: ay, there's the rub;
For in that sleep of death what dreams may come
When we have shuffled off this mortal coil,
Must give us pause: there's the respect
That makes calamity of so long life;
For who would bear the whips and scorns of time,
The oppressor's wrong, the proud man's contumely,
The pangs of despised love, the law's delay,
The insolence of office and the spurns
That patient merit of the unworthy takes,
When he himself might his quietus make
With a bare bodkin? who would fardels bear,
To grunt and sweat under a weary life,
But that the dread of something after death,
The undiscover'd country from whose bourn
No traveller returns, puzzles the will
And makes us rather bear those ills we have
Than fly to others that we know not of?
Thus conscience does make cowards of us all;

And thus the native hue of resolution
Is sicklied o'er with the pale cast of thought,
And enterprises of great pith and moment
With this regard their currents turn awry,
And lose the name of action. —Soft you now!
The fair Ophelia! Nymph, in thy orisons
Be all my sins remember'd.

Text D   Of Studies

Read the following passage and finish the following exercises.
1) The following essay is from the work _____, which was written by _____.
2) "Studies serve for delight, for ornament, and for ability."
   How do you understand the statement above? Share your understanding with your classmates.
3) To spend too much time in studies is _____; to use them too much for ornament, is _____; to make judgment wholly by their rules, is the _____ of a scholar.
4) Crafty men _____ studies, simple men _____ them, and wise men _____ them.
   ① use   ② contemn   ③ admire
5) Some books are to be _____, others to be _____, and some few to be _____ and digested.
6) Reading maketh a _____ man; conference a _____ man; and writing an _____ man.
   ① ready   ② exact   ③ full

Studies serve for delight, for ornament, and for ability. Their chief use for delight, is in privateness and retiring; for ornament, is in discourse; and for ability, is in the judgment, and disposition of business. For expert men can execute, and perhaps judge of particulars, one by one; but the general counsels, and the plots and marshalling of affairs, come best, from those that are learned.

To spend too much time in studies is sloth; to use them too much for ornament is affectation; to make judgment wholly by their rules, is the humor of a scholar. They perfect nature, and are perfected by experience: for natural abilities are like natural plants, that need pruning, by study; and studies themselves, do give forth directions too much at large, except they be bounded in by experience.

Crafty men contemn studies, simple men admire them, and wise men use them; for they teach not their own use; but that is a wisdom without them, and above them, won by observation. Read not to contradict and confute; nor to believe and take for granted; nor to find talk and discourse; but to weigh and consider.

Some books are to be tasted, others to be swallowed, and some few to be chewed and digested; that is, some books are to be read only in parts; others to be read, but not curiously; and some few to be read wholly, and with diligence and attention. Some books also may be read by deputy, and extracts made of them by others; but that would be only in the less important arguments, and the meaner sort of books, else distilled books are like common distilled waters, flashy things.

Reading maketh a full man; conference a ready man; and writing an exact man. And therefore, if a man write little, he had need have a great memory; if he confer little, he had need have a present wit; and if he read little, he had need have much cunning, to seem to know, that he doth not. Histories make men wise; poets witty; the mathematics subtle; natural philosophy deep; moral grave; logic and rhetoric able to contend.

Nay, there is no stand or impediment in the wit, but may be wrought out by fit studies; like as diseases of the body, may have appropriate exercises. Bowling is good for the stone and reins; shooting for the lungs and breast; gentle walking for the stomach; riding for the head; and the like. So if a man's wit be wandering, let him study the mathematics; for in demonstrations, if his wit be called away never so little, he must begin again. If his wit be not apt to distinguish or find differences, let him study the schoolmen; for they are cymini sectores; if he be not apt to beat over matters, and to call up one thing to prove and illustrate another, let him study the lawyers' cases. So every defect of the mind, may have a special receipt.

For Fun

Books to read

Gulliver's Travels by Jonathan Swift—An Englishman returns after a long time abroad and tells his strange stories about the lands he visited which are allegories about the real world.

Robinson Crusoe by Daniel Defoe—The classical story of Robinson Crusoe, a man who is dragged to a desert island after a shipwreck. . .

Movies to see

Cleopatra—Historical epic. The triumphs and tragedy of the Egyptian queen, Cleopatra.

Shakespeare in Love—The young Shakespeare, out of ideas and short of cash, meets his ideal woman and is inspired to write one of his most famous plays.

Poem to appreciate

A Red Red Rose

By Robert Burns

O my Luve's like a red, red rose
That's newly sprung in June;
O my Luve's like the melodie
That's sweetly played in tune.

As fair art thou, my bonnie lass,
So deep in luve am I;
And I will luve thee still, my dear,
Till a' the seas gang dry:

Till a' the seas gang dry, my dear,
And the rocks melt wi' the sun;
I will luve thee still, my dear,
While the sands o' life shall run.

And fare thee weel, my only Luve,
And fare thee weel awhile!
And I will come again, my Luve,
Tho' it ware ten thousand mile.

Unit 15
The British Literature (II)

> I am never long, even in the society of her I love, without yearning for the company of my lamp and my library.
>
> —Lord Byron
>
> Beneath the rule of men entirely great, / The pen is mightier than the sword.
>
> —G. K. Chesterton

Unit Goals

- To have a general view of British literature
- To get acquainted with some famous British writers and their works
- To develop critical thinking and intercultural communication skills
- To learn useful words and expressions concerning British literature and improve English language skills

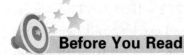

Before You Read

Test your knowledge in British literature. Match the classic lines with the works.

① "Do you think I can stay to become nothing to you? Do you think I am an automaton? A machine without feelings? ... Do you think, because I am poor, obscure, plain, and little, I am soulless and heartless? You think wrong!"

② I wandered lonely as a cloud / That floats on high o'er vales and hills...

③ He rose from the table; and advancing to the master, basin and spoon in hand, said somewhat alarmed at his own temerity: "Please, sir, I want some more."

④ His fists were shut, his mouth set fast. He would not take that direction, to the darkness, to follow her. He walked towards the faintly humming, glowing town, quickly.

⑤ It is a truth universally acknowledged, that a single man in possession of a good fortune

英国国情 英国社会与文化(第3版)

must be in want of a wife.

⑥ If Winter comes, can Spring be far behind?

_____ "Daffodils"   _____ Oliver Twist

_____ Pride and Prejudice   _____ "Ode to the West Wind"

_____ Jane Eyre   _____ Sons and Lovers

Start to Read

Text A   Overview of British Literature (II)

The Romantic Period

1 **Roughly** the first third of the 19th century makes up English literature's romantic period. Writers of romantic literature are more **concerned** with imagination and feeling than with the power of reason which marked the 18th century. Perhaps the rather violent and ugly world about them drove 19th century writers to a literary **refuge**.

Romantic Poets

2 In 1798, a volume of poems was published in London under the title *Lyrical Ballads*, which was also called romantic poetry's Declaration of Independence. It made literary history, for it **contained** the poems of two

William Wordsworth

young men who wrote about new subjects in a new poetical language. The two men were William Wordsworth (1770—1850) and Samuel Taylor Coleridge (1772—1834). They were then living in the Lake District, and hence they were called the "Lakers." Wordsworth stands for **dominant** ideas in poetry, the poetry of nature and the poetry of **simplicity**, and his treatment of nature is the most wonderful of its kind in English literature. Among his most famous poems are "Lucy Gray," "Daffodils" and so on. His friend Coleridge wrote such poems as "Kubla Khan" and "The Rime of Ancient Mariner." He represented the mysterious and exotic side of romanticism.

3 Three young men brought the Romantic Movement to its **height**. They were Byron, Shelley and Keats. George Gordon Byron (1788—1824) traveled widely in Europe, part of the time an exile because of **scandals** related to his

---
166

marriage. At the age of 36, he died of a fever in Greece, where he had gone as a **volunteer** to fight for Greek independence. Byron wrote many works, but *Don Juan*, the long **satirical** epic, is generally considered his masterpiece. Percy Bysshe Shelley (1792—1822) is mostly known for his "Ode to the West Wind," whose ending "If winter comes, can spring be far behind?" has given courage to many revolutionaries faced with reverses, even death. Besides, he wrote many other notable works, such as the lyrical drama *Prometheus Unbound*. John Keats (1795—1821) died young at the age of 26. He wrote some of the most beautiful odes in the English language, such as "Ode to a Nightingale," "Ode on a Grecian Urn" and so on.

Novelists

4 Jane Austen (1775—1817) is often called the last of the 18th century novelists because of her **crisp**, controlled studies of manners. The novel of manners pictures in detail the manners and customs of a certain social class. Jane Austen, who excelled at this form of writing, is indeed one of the greatest of all English novelists. A delightful, almost **flawless** stylist, she has devoted admirers of her *Sense and Sensibility*, *Pride and Prejudice*, *Emma*, and *Northanger Abbey*, among other works.

5 The romantic period knows no more **fascinating** literary family than the Brontës. Their work stands apart and is hard to **classify**. Three daughters of an Irish-born clergyman grew up at Haworth parsonage in Yorkshire. This remote region of **bleak** moors greatly influenced the imagination of the sisters, Charlotte, Emily and Anne. Anne Brontë (1820—1849) is the least important of the three and her chief novel is *Agnes Grey*. Charlotte Brontë (1816—1855) produced *Jane Eyre*, an exciting novel that is partly **autobiographical**. The masterpiece of Emily Brontë (1818—1848) is *Wuthering Heights*, which won her lasting fame and made her one of the few greatest English novelists.

Victorian Literature

6 The romantic period **shades** gradually into the Victorian age, which takes its name from Queen Victoria. She came to throne in 1837 and reigned until 1901. The romantic spirit did not disappear, but it ceased to be a clearly leading influence. This period saw modern kinds of realistic writing and some authors who showed a new, deeper understanding of character.

7 Two figures **tower over** the Victorian novel. William Makepeace

Thackeray (1811—1863) is a master of satire, a critic of what he thought false in life. Most of his characters and plots come from upper-and-middle-class life. His masterwork is *Vanity Fair*, and its heroine, Becky Sharp is one of the **immoral**

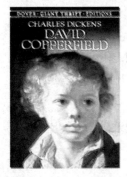

personalities of English fiction. But in the creation of memorable characters, Thackeray is topped by Charles Dickens (1812—1870). After a boyhood of poverty, partly reflected in his own favorite book, *David Copperfield*, Dickens became a man of wealth through his books. His novels **combine** a rare comic gift—especially in Pickwick Papers, his earliest success—and a power to reduce his readers to tears. Some of the books, such as *Oliver Twist*,

Great Expectations and *A Tale of Two Cities* also enjoy great popularity among the readers.

8 George Eliot (1819—1880), whose real name was Mary Ann Evans, combines great narrative power and **depth** of thought. As a scholar and philosopher her powers **outreach** those of Dickens and Thackeray. *Adam Bede*, *The Mill on the Floss* and *Silas Marner* give expert pictures of the working class and their experiences. *Middlemarch* is Eliot's masterpiece, which presents the theme of **incompatibility** in marriage.

9 Oscar Wilde (1854—1900) possessed a wealth of talents. He was a poet of **distinction** ("The Ballad of Reading Gaol"), story writer ("The Happy Prince"), and novelist (*The Picture of Dorian Gray*). Perhaps most important of all, he was a playwright. His writing for the theatre ranged from the poetic drama *Salome* to a series of sparkling, witty comedies such as *The Importance of Being Earnest*.

10 Thomas Hardy (1840—1928) lived well into the 20th century but did his major work as a novelist in the 19th century. Representative of his work are *The Return of the Native*, *Tess of the D'Urbervilles*, and *Jude the Obscure*. These books fall into the prose group that Hardy called novels of character and environment.

The First Half of 20th Century

11 Many traits of Victorian literature carried over until World War I began in 1914. But during the early years of the 20th century, new ideas in writing were mixed with the old, to follow the changing times.

12 William Butler Yeats (1865—1939) from Ireland, poet and playwright, led a group of his countrymen in a **vigorous revival** of Irish culture. Some of his best lyrics were published in *Poems*. Yeats helped found Dublin's Abbey

Theatre, which performed many of his verse plays, including *At the Hawk's Well*. In 1923, he received the Nobel Prize for literature.

13 Of all the **prominent** writers active both before and after World War I, George Bernard Shaw (1856—1950) **looms** as the giant. His comic talents and **immense** output probably earn this brilliant Irishman the rank of leading English-Language playwright after Shakespeare. His wit and satire have held the stages of the world in such plays as *Man and Superman*, *Major Barbara*, *Pygmalion* and *Mrs. Warren's Profession*. To Shaw, nothing was sacred. Marriage, religion and parenthood received the same acid treatment as social **snobbery** and politics.

14 Of the 20th century novelists, few are more **impressive** than Joseph Conrad (1857—1924). Polish-born, Conrad was in his twenties before he knew any English. After becoming a British subject, he wrote brilliant novels in his **adopted** tongue. Among them are *Lord Jim* and *The Heart of Darkness*.

15 The novels of E. M. Forster (1879—1970) concern themselves with personal relations. His novels *A Room with a View* and *Howards End* established his **reputation** as one of England's most important writers. In his most notable book, *A Passage to India*, Forster examined the relationships between English-men and Indians.

16 New generations of fiction writers followed. They **experimented** with new forms and made use of new insights into character as modern **psychology** developed. They challenged old ideas and made known their fresh ideas about life and art.

17 James Joyce (1882—1941) is regarded as one of the leading writers of modern times. He introduced **startling** new forms into the novel and was the first to make major use of stream of consciousness—the free flow of language revealing one person's thoughts, feelings and memories. *Ulysses* gives a **striking**, detailed picture of one day in the lives of Leopold Bloom and Stephen Dedalus.

18 D. H. Lawrence (1885—1930) felt that society forced too many rules on people and kept them from living a full, natural life. Lawrence's forceful writing on daring themes shocked many. *Sons and Lovers*, based partly on his own life, is one of his finest novels.

19 Several gifted women have added to the quality of 20th century fiction. Virginia Woolf (1882—1941) experimented **constantly**, always refining her special form of writing. She was less interested in plot than in probing people's characters, experiences and feelings. Many

consider *The Waves* her best novel. The **delicate**, beautifully written short stories of Katherine Mansfield (1888—1923) have a surprising strength about them. In *Bliss* and *The Garden Party*, story after story perfectly **captures** a single emotion or **dramatic** event.

After You Read

Knowledge Focus

1. Match the following literary works with the correspondent writers.

1) Charles Dickens	a. *Vanity Fair*
2) George Eliot	b. *The Mill on the Floss*
3) D. H. Lawrence	c. *Pygmalion*
4) Emily Bronte	d. *Tess of the D'Urbervilles*
5) Virginia Woolf	e. *Great Expectations*
6) Bernard Shaw	f. *The Waves*
7) William Thackeray	g. *Sons and Lovers*
8) Thomas Hardy	h. *Wuthering Heights*

2. Match the following writers with the correspondent descriptions of them.

1) George Bernard Shaw	7) William Wordsworth
2) George Gordon Byron	8) James Joyce
3) William Thackeray	9) Samuel Taylor Coleridge
4) Oscar Wilde	10) Jane Austen
5) John Keats	11) Joseph Conrad
6) Virginia Woolf	12) D. H. Lawrence

A. They were then living in the Lake District, and they were called the "Lakers."

B. At the age of 36, he died of a fever in Greece, where he had gone as a volunteer to fight for Greek independence.

C. He died young at the age of 26. He wrote some of the most beautiful odes in the English language

D. She is often called the last of the 18th century novelists because of her crisp, controlled studies of manners.

E. He is a master of satire, a critic of what he thought false in life. Most of his characters and plots come from upper-and-middle class life.

F. He possessed a wealth of talents. He was a poet of distinction, story writer, and novelist. Perhaps most important of all, he was a playwright.

G. His comic talents and immense output probably earn this brilliant Irishman the rank of leading English-Language playwright after Shakespeare.

H. Polish-born, he was in his twenties before he knew any English. After becoming a British subject, he wrote brilliant novels in his adopted tongue.

I. He introduced startling new forms into the novel and was the first to make major use of stream of consciousness.

J. He felt that society forced too many rules on people and kept them from living a full, natural life. His forceful writing on daring themes shocked many.

K. She was less interested in plot than in probing people's characters, experiences and feelings.

Language Focus

1. **Complete the following sentences with proper words and expressions.**

roughly	dramatic	loom	exotic
experiment	capture	striking	outreach
tower over	adopt	immense	shade

1) The coming examination _____ larger with every passing day.

2) The novel _____ the imagination of thousands of readers.

3) It's almost impossible to find him in the _____ ocean.

4) _____ speaking, I would say that about 100 people attended the exhibition.

5) There were some _____ similarities between the two books.

6) New methods of teaching foreign languages are _____ in this institute.

7) The conversation stopped when she made her _____ entrance.

8) Its colour was a sort of blue, but now it has _____ off into grey.

9) The film retains much of the book's _____ flavour.

10) She had to _____ her opponent to win the fencing match.

11) How maddening to have your younger brother _____ you, at his age, too!

12) Is it right to _____ on animals?

2. **Complete the following sentences with the words given in proper forms.**

1) The _____ (simple) of the book makes it suitable for children.

2) There are many _____ (mystery) stories about the Egyptian pyramids.

3) Overall, the tone of the book is _____ (satire) in tone.

4) He displayed a _____ (flaw) technique in the competition.

5) Using other people for one's own profit is _____ (moral).

6) The book is _____ (fascinate), despite its uninspiring title.

7) We had a _____ (memory) trip last year.

8) We should make a _____ (distinct) between right and wrong.

9) The _____ (revive) of our country depends on our young generation.

10) Is his distance a result of _____ (snob) or shyness?

11) Though nearly 50, he was exceptionally _____ (vigor) in work.

12) The government is alarmed by the _____ (drama) increase in violent crime.

3. **Proofreading and error correction.**

The passage contains FIVE errors. Each indicated line contains a maximum of ONE error.
In each case, only ONE word is involved.

D. H. Lawrencewas one of the greatest English novelist of the twentieth century. He was a very original, but also a very controversial writer. He wrote chiefly the relationship between parents and children, the passion between men and women, the ugliness, mammonism, sham morality of modern industrialized society. His well-known short poem "How Beastly the Bourgeois Is" shows his strong disgust with the bourgeois society of his time. "My great religion," he wrote in 1913, "is a belief in the blood, the flesh, as being wise than the intellect." He denounced the "artificial complexities of civilization." He spent much of his life expose the evils of modern society, but could not find a way to help solve its many problems.

1) _____

2) _____

3) _____

4) _____

5) _____

Comprehensive Work

1. Group Work: Work in groups and wind up the unfinished story.

A man wearing a heavy army jacket, a pullover wool cap, and dark sunglasses walked into the Bank at the corner of Maple and Main streets in downtown.

The man walked up to the teller and held up a hand grenade for all to see. He said, "Give me all your money, all the money in this bank, right now!"

Everyone in the lobby screamed and started running, even the security guard. Nervously, the young female teller handed the man three big bags loaded with cash...

(*To be continued*)

2. Essay Writing

Write a passage of about 300 words, presenting your understanding of the following questions.

❖ What is your favorite English novel?

❖ Why do you love it?

Read More

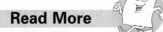

Text B   Pride and Prejudice

Read the following passage and finish the following exercises.

1) Fill in the blanks with given words in their proper forms.

   Although first published almost 200 years ago, the novels of Jane Austen have retained their _____ (popular) around the world. It is not difficult to find the reasons for their _____ (endure) appeal.

2) Austen wrote about universal themes, such as the joy and pain of _____, the pursuit of _____, and the need to be accepted by society.

3) The plot of *Pride and Prejudice* revolves mainly around _____, and her troublesome romance with the wealthy but arrogant _____.

4) Sort the following characters into different teams according to their relations.

Elizabeth	Bingley	Lydia	Mr. Bennet
Darcy	Wickham	Jane	Caroline

a. Father & Daughters:

   _____

b. Sisters:

   _____

c. Brother & Sister:

   _____

d. Lovers:

   _____

  Although first published almost 200 years ago, the novels of Jane Austen have retained their popularity around the world. It is not difficult to find the reasons for their enduring appeal. Austen wrote about universal themes, such as the joy and pain of love, the pursuit of happiness, and the need to be accepted by society.

  Jane Austen was born in 1775 in a rural part of southern England. She and her family were all avid readers. They even read novels, which were often looked down on during that time. Jane began writing before her teens, and had completed a history book by the time she was sixteen.

  The six romantic novels that Austen wrote before her death in 1817 are still widely read. Her first novel published was *Sense and Sensibility* in 1811, but her best-known work, *Pride and Prejudice*, was written around fifteen years earlier. Although originally rejected for publication, the novel, and its intelligent heroine, have come to hold a place among the great classics of English literature.

Pride and Prejudice tells the story of Mr. and Mrs. Bennet, a somewhat absurd couple, and their five young, unmarried daughters. The plot revolves mainly around the second daughter, Elizabeth, and her troublesome romance with the wealthy but arrogant Mr. Darcy. Mr. Darcy represents the pride of the novel's title, while the prejudice is represented by Elizabeth's attitude toward Mr. Darcy. In the novel, Elizabeth must overcome her prejudice against him before she can fall in love.

Elizabeth's romance with Mr. Darcy parallels that of her older sister Jane with his friend, Charles Bingley. Jane's relationship starts off much more smoothly, and survives the efforts of Bingley's unpleasant sister, Caroline, to break it up. Other significant subplots include the adventures of Lydia, the youngest Bennet daughter. She brings disgrace on the family by running away with a man named Wickham.

Everything ends well, of course. Even Wickham ends up marrying Lydia. Jane and Charles get married. So do Elizabeth and Mr. Darcy, once he has overcome his dislike of the Bennet family's strange ways, and she has seen the decent man behind the pride.

"I must confess that I think her as delightful a character as ever appeared in print, and how I shall be able to tolerate those who do not like her at least, I do not know." In the flowery language of the early 19th century, that was how Jane Austen described her character Elizabeth Bennet in a letter to a friend.

Jane Austen need not have feared. Elizabeth has probably attracted more sympathy and admiration than any other of the author's characters, male or female. She is a lively, quick-witted young woman with a strong sense of justice and a natural goodness that have widespread appeal.

One of the most interesting moments in *Pride and Prejudice* comes when Elizabeth reluctantly visits Darcy's home, and perceives the high respect in which he is held by everyone around him. It is the turning point of the story, when she begins to see beyond Darcy's pride and develop real feelings for him. It also shows Jane Austen's skill at dealing with complex emotions and timeless themes in her deceptively simple stories.

Text C   Christmas Dinner

(Excerpted from *Great Expectations*)

Read the following passage and finish the following exercises.

1) The novel *Great Expectations* was written by _____.
2) From the passage we can know that "My" name is _____, and Joe is "my" _____.
3) "My sister went for the stone bottle, came back with the stone bottle, and poured his brandy out: no one else taking any. The wretched man trifled with his glass—took it up, looked at it through the light, put it down—prolonged my misery."
Why did "I" feel so nervous when Mr. Pumblechook was about to drink the brandy?

Joe offered me more gravy, which I was afraid to take.

"He was a world of trouble to you, ma'am," said Mrs. Hubble, commiserating my sister.

"Trouble?" echoed my sister; "trouble?" and then entered on a fearful catalogue of all the illnesses I had been guilty of, and all the acts of sleeplessness I had committed, and all the high places I had tumbled from, and all the low places I had tumbled into, and all the injuries I had done myself, and all the times she had wished me in my grave, and I had contumaciously refused to go there.

I think the Romans must have aggravated one another very much, with their noses. Perhaps, they became the restless people they were, in consequence. Anyhow, Mr. Wopsle's Roman nose so aggravated me, during the recital of my misdemeanours, that I should have liked to pull it until he howled. But, all I had endured up to this time, was nothing in comparison with the awful feelings that took possession of me when the pause was broken which ensued upon my sister's recital, and in which pause everybody had looked at me (as I felt painfully conscious) with indignation and abhorrence.

"Yet," said Mr. Pumblechook, leading the company gently back to the theme from which they had strayed, "Pork—regarded as biled—is rich, too; ain't it?"

"Have a little brandy, uncle," said my sister.

O Heavens, it had come at last! He would find it was weak, he would say it was weak, and I was lost! I held tight to the leg of the table under the cloth, with both hands, and awaited my fate.

My sister went for the stone bottle, came back with the stone bottle, and poured his brandy out: no one else taking any. The wretched man trifled with his glass—took it up, looked at it through the light, put it down—prolonged my misery. All this time, Mrs. Joe and Joe were briskly clearing the table for the pie and pudding.

I couldn't keep my eyes off him. Always holding tight by the leg of the table with my hands and feet, I saw the miserable creature finger his glass playfully, take it up, smile, throw his head back, and drink the brandy off. Instantly afterwards, the company were seized with unspeakable consternation, owing to his springing to his feet, turning round several times in an appalling spasmodic whooping-cough dance, and rushing out at the door; he then became visible through the window, violently plunging and expectorating, making the most hideous faces, and apparently out of his mind.

I held on tight, while Mrs. Joe and Joe ran to him. I didn't know how I had done it, but I had no doubt I had murdered him somehow. In my dreadful situation, it was a relief when he was brought back, and, surveying the company all round as if they had disagreed with him, sank down into his chair with the one significant gasp, "Tar!"

I had filled up the bottle from the tar-water jug. I knew he would be worse by-and-by. I moved the table, like a Medium of the present day, by the vigour of my unseen hold upon it.

"Tar!" cried my sister, in amazement. "Why, how ever could Tar come there?"

But, Uncle Pumblechook, who was omnipotent in that kitchen, wouldn't hear the word, wouldn't hear of the subject, imperiously waved it all away with his hand, and asked for hot gin-and-water. My sister, who had begun to be alarmingly meditative, had to employ herself actively in getting the gin, the hot water, the sugar, and the lemon-peel, and mixing them. For the time being at least, I was saved. I still held on to the leg of the table, but clutched it now with the fervour of gratitude.

By degrees, I became calm enough to release my grasp and partake of pudding. Mr. Pumblechook partook of pudding. All partook of pudding. The course terminated, and Mr. Pumblechook had begun to beam under the genial influence of gin-and-water. I began to think I should get over the day, when my sister said to Joe, "Clean plates—cold."

I clutched the leg of the table again immediately, and pressed it to my bosom as if it had been the companion of my youth and friend of my soul. I foresaw what was coming, and I felt that this time I really was gone.

"You must taste," said my sister, addressing the guests with her best grace, "You must taste, to finish with, such a delightful and delicious present of Uncle Pumblechook's!"

Must they! Let them not hope to taste it!

"You must know," said my sister, rising, "it's a pie; a savoury pork pie."

The company murmured their compliments. Uncle Pumblechook, sensible of having deserved well of his fellow-creatures, said—quite vivaciously, all things considered— "Well, Mrs. Joe, we'll do our best endeavours; let us have a cut at this same pie."

My sister went out to get it. I heard her steps proceed to the pantry. I saw Mr. Pumblechook balance his knife. I saw re-awakening appetite in the Roman nostrils of Mr. Wopsle. I heard Mr. Hubble remark that "a bit of savoury pork pie would lay atop of anything you could mention, and do no harm," and I heard Joe say, "You shall have some, Pip." I have never been absolutely certain whether I uttered a shrill yell of terror, merely in spirit, or in the bodily hearing of the company. I felt that I could bear no more, and that I must run away. I released the leg of the table, and ran for my life.

Text D   Agatha Christie—Queen of Crime

Read the following passage and finish the following exercises.

1) Agatha Christie is a prolific English author of _____ stories.
   a. detective   b. children's   c. romantic
2) Which of the following characters is NOT created by Agatha Christie? _____
   a. Hercule Poirot   b. Sherlock Holmes   c. Miss Jane Marple
3) Which of the following stories is NOT written by Agatha Christie? _____
   a. *Death on the Nile* b. *Murder on the Orient Express*
   c. *A Study in Scarlet*

Dame Agatha Christie (1890—1976), prolific English "Queen of Crime," author of world-renown created such famous detectives as Hercule Poirot, the eccentric Belgian who relied on his keen grasp of logic to nab crooks;

> Crime is terribly revealing. Try and vary your methods as you will, your tastes, your habits, your attitude of mind, and your soul is revealed by your actions.
>
> —Poirot, in *The ABC Murders* Ch. 17

and English spinster Miss Jane Marple (partly inspired by her maternal grandmother) who used her feminine intuition to solve crime. Her motto:

> "The young people think the old people are fools, but the old people *know* the young people are fools."

Some of Christie's best-known works are *The ABC Murders* (1936), *And Then There Were None* (1945), *The Mousetrap* (longest ever running stage play in London, first performed in 1952), *Hickory Dickory Dock* (1955), *Witness for the Prosecution* (1957), *Murder on the Orient Express* (1974), and *Death on the Nile* (1978). From her first novel *The Mysterious Affair at Styles* (1920) to her last, *Sleeping Murder* (1976), Christie enjoyed a career that spanned over fifty years and her works have now sold into the billions. They have been translated to dozens of languages, inspired numerous other authors' works, and have been adapted to radio, the stage, and film. As well as a writer of crime mysteries, she also read stories for BBC Radio, wrote non-fiction, romances, plays, and poetry.

Born in the family home Ashfield in Torquay, Devon, England on 15 September 1890, Agatha Mary Clarissa Miller was the youngest of the three children born to Clarissa "Clara" Margaret née Boehmer (1855—1926) and American Frederick Alvah Miller (1846—1901), who died when Agatha was just ten years old. The shy and sensitive Agatha, who was very close to her mother, had an older sister, Margaret "Madge" (1879—1950) and brother Louis "Monty" Montant (1880—1929). The family attended All Saint's Church where Agatha was baptised. While she received no formal education, her mother and then governesses taught her at home to read before she entered finishing school in Paris, France in 1906. Having long been encouraged by her mother to write, Agatha continued to write there while also studying music (which became a life-long love), singing, and piano.

On December 24, 1914, at the age of twenty-four, Christie married Royal Flying Corps pilot Archie Christie, with whom she would have a daughter, Rosalind (1919—2004). During WWI Agatha worked as a nurse, tending the ill and injured, many of whom were displaced Belgians. Their bewilderment and personal sorrows affected her deeply. She amassed a great deal of knowledge about sicknesses and poisons such as strychnine and ricin that she often featured in her novels. Around this time she also started writing her first novel *The Mysterious Affair at Styles*, an immediate best-seller. In 1926, profoundly grieving the death of her mother, Christie created some mystery of her own, disappearing for a time; when she was found, she claimed that she had had a bout of amnesia.

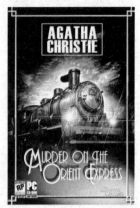

In 1928, Archie divorced Agatha. She then set off on her first of many trips to the Middle East, traveling on the famed Orient Express from Calais, France to Baghdad, Iraq, then on to the ancient city of Ur in Mesopotamia. It was on her second trip there she met her future husband, archaeologist Sir Max Edgar Lucien Mallowan (1904—1978). They were married in Scotland on 11 September 1930. She often accompanied him on digs as a member of the team, photographing and cataloguing finds. In 1960 Max was honoured as Commander of the British Empire (CBE) and in 1968 knighted for his archaeological work.

Christie herself won many awards and honours in her life-time including: 1955, received the Mystery Writers of America Grand Master award; 1961, awarded an honorary degree from Exeter University; 1967, became president of The British Detection Club; 1971, received England's highest honor, the Order of the British Empire, Dame Commander.

In 1974 Christie appeared for the last time in public on opening night for her play *Murder on the Orient Express*. When she was not traveling the world, her and Max's home in England was in the town of Wallingford, Oxfordshire, where she died peacefully on 12 January 1976. Max survived her by two years. They now rest together in the Parish Church cemetery of St. Mary's in Cholsey, Oxfordshire.

> I have enjoyed greatly the second blooming that comes when you finish the life of the emotions and of personal relations; and suddenly you find—at the age of fifty, say— that a whole new life has opened before you, filled with things you can think about, study, or read about... It is as if a fresh sap of ideas and thoughts was rising in you.
>
> —*An Autobiography* (1977)

For Fun

Books to read

Great Expectations by Charles Dickens—the story of the orphan Pip, tracing his life from his early days of childhood until adulthood.

A Mill on the Floss by George Eliot—Lawyer Wakem takes away the mill on the river Floss from Edward Tulliver, whose ancestors owned it for 300 years...

A Room with a View by E. M. Forster—Set in Italy and England, the story is both a romance and a critique of English society at the beginning of the 20th century.

Movies to see

The Importance of Being Earnest—In the 1890s London, two friends use the same pseudonym ("Ernest") for their on-the-sly activities. Hilarity ensues.

Becoming Jane—A biographical portrait of a pre-fame Jane Austen and her romance with a young Irishman.

Death on the Nile—Agatha Christie's Hercule Poirot has a set of murder suspects on a boat in the Nile after a rich heiress is killed. Can he find the culprit before they reach port?

重点参考书目和网站

[1] McClean，D. & K. B. Morris（2005）．*The Conflict of Laws*. 6th edition. London：Sweet & Maxwell Ltd.

[2] Olmert，M.（1996）．*Milton's Teeth and Ovid's Umbrella*：*Curiouser & Curiouser Adventures in History*. Simon & Schuster，New York.

[3] Raphael，D. D.，D. Limon，and W. R. McKay（2004）．*Erskine May*：*Parliamentary Practice*，23rd ed. London：Butterworths Tolley.

[4] DeMaria，R.（2001）．*British Literature 1640—1789*：*An Anthology*，Blackwell Publishing.

[5] Slapper，G, and D. Kelly（2008）．*The English Legal System*. London：Routledge-Cavendish.

[6] Spencer，C.（2003）．*British Food*：*An Extraordinary Thousand Years of History*. Columbia University Press.

[7] Sutton，D.（2000）．*A chorus of raspberries*：*British film comedy 1929—1939*. Exeter：University of Exeter Press.

[8] 高继海.（2006）．简明英国文学史[M]．开封：河南大学出版社.

[9] 姜志伟，罗德喜，李啸.（2004）．大学英语——英美文化链接[Z]．北京：中国书籍出版社.

[10] 孔翔兰，赵东林，张菊荣.（2007）．西方文化风情路——英国篇[M]．西安：西北工业大学出版社.

[11] 刘晓萊.（2005）．英语国家社会与文化[M]．北京：中国电力出版社.

[12] 钱清.（2006）．礼仪与风俗[Z]．北京：外文出版社.

[13] 泰瑞·陈.（2008）．文化震撼之旅——英国[M]．孙丽冰 译 北京：旅游教育出版社.

[14] 图仁.（2006）．大国细节——英国[M]．南京：凤凰出版传媒集团/江苏文艺出版社.

[15] 王虹.（2003）.当代英国社会与文化[M]．上海：上海外语教育出版社.

[16] 汪榕培，任秀桦.（1996）英语学习背景知识词典[M]．上海：上海外语教育出版社.

[17] 王微萍.（2005）．实用英国文化知识200问[M]．重庆：重庆大学出版社.

[18] 吴斐.（2003）．英国社会与文化[M]．武昌：武汉大学出版社.

[19] 肖惠云.（2003）．当代英国概况[M]．上海：上海外语教育出版社.朱永涛.（1991）英美文化基础教程[M]．北京：外语教学与研究出版社.

[20] 朱永涛，王立礼.（2000）．英语国家社会与文化入门[M]．北京：高等教育出版社.

[21] 朱昱，代芊.（2006）．节日与婚礼[Z]．北京：外文出版社.

[22] 朱振武，白岸杨，江先发.（2006）．英语夜读15分钟——经典[Z]．上海：上海译文出版社.

[23] 朱振武，张柯，陈慧莲.（2006）．英语夜读15分钟——时文[Z]．上海：上海译文出版社.

[24] 朱振武，赵永健，信艳.（2006）．英语夜读15分钟——文化[Z]．上海：上海译文出版社.

[25] 欧美文化：http://www.zftrans.com/bbs/thread.php? fid = 26

[26] BBC 英语教学频道：http://www.english.hsw.cn/

[27] 英语资料：http://www.en8848.com.cn/yingyu/36/category-catid-936.html

[28] All about British Life and Culture：http://www.projectbritain.com/

[29] Choose British：http://www.choosebritish.co.uk/

[30] Study，Work or Travel in the UK. British Culture and Life：http://www.ukstudentlife.com/index.htm

[31] BBC World News：http://www.hxen.com/englishlistening/bbc/

[32] Higher Education System：http://www.polytech.poltava.ua/education/america/usa_3.html

[33] Wales Society and Culture：http://www.bbc.co.uk/wales/culture/

[34] United Kingdom Travel：http://www.gouk.about.com/

[35] Music Videos and Lyrics：http://www.musicloversgroup.com/emigrate-new-york-city-lyrics-and-

video/

[36] Culture of the United Kingdom：http：//www. en. wikipedia. org/wiki/Culture_of_the_United_ Kingdom

[37] British Culture，British Customs and British Traditions：http：//www. learnenglish. de/ britishculture. htm

[38] Wikipedia，the Free Encyclopedia：http：//www. en. wikipedia. org/wiki/

[39] Kate Fox. (2004). *Watching the English：The Hidden Rules of English Behaviour*. London：Hodder & Stoughton.

[40] John Henry Newman. (2008) *The Idea of a University Defined and Illustrated：In Nine Discourses Delivered to the Catholics of Dublin*. http：//www. gutenberg. org/license

[41] Michael Higgins，Clarissa Smith & John Storey. (2010) *The Cambridge Companion to Modern British Culture*. Cambridge：Cambridge University Press.

[42] Peter Childs & Mike Storry. (1999). *Encyclopedia of Contemporary British Culture*. London & New York：Routledge.

[43] Peter Thomson. (2008). *The Cambridge History of British Theatre*. Cambridge：Cambridge University Press.

《英国国情：英国社会与文化》（第3版）

尊敬的老师：

您好！

为了方便您更好地使用本教材，获得最佳教学效果，我们特向使用该书作为教材的教师赠送本教材配套课件资料。如有需要，请完整填写"教师联系表"并加盖所在单位系（院）公章，免费向出版社索取。

北京大学出版社

✂ ···

教 师 联 系 表

教材名称	《英国国情：英国社会与文化》（第3版）			
姓名：	性别：		职务：	职称：
E-mail：		联系电话：	邮政编码：	
供职学校：		所在院系：		（章）
学校地址：				
教学科目与年级：			班级人数：	
通信地址：				

填写完毕后，请将此表邮寄给我们，我们将为您免费寄送本教材配套资料，谢谢！

北京市海淀区成府路 205 号

北京大学出版社外语编辑部　李　颖

邮政编码：100871

电子邮箱：evalee1770@sina.com

邮 购 部 电 话：010-62534449

市场营销部电话：010-62750672

外语编辑部电话：010-62754382